Artillery Hell

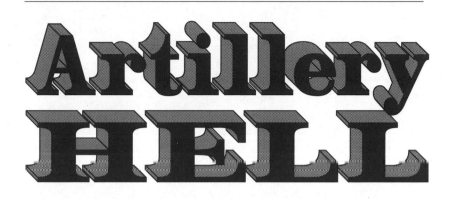

The Employment of Artillery
at Antietam

Curt Johnson and Richard C. Anderson, Jr.

with the 1940 report by
Joseph Mills Hanson

Foreword by Edwin C. Bearss

Texas A&M University Press
COLLEGE STATION

Library of Congress Cataloging-in-Publication Data

Johnson, Curt.
    Artillery hell : the employment of artillery at An-
tietam / by Curt Johnson and Richard C. Anderson, Jr. ;
with the 1940 report by Joseph Mills Hanson ; foreword by Edwin C. Bearss.—1st ed.
      p. cm.—(Texas A & M University military his-
tory series : no. 36)
    Includes bibliographical references and index.
    ISBN 0-89096-622-2 (cloth).
    ISBN 0-89096-623-0 (paper).
    1. Antietam, Battle of, Md., 1862. 2. United States—
History—Civil War, 1861–1865—Artillery operations.
I. Anderson, Richard C. (Richard Claire), 1955– .
II. Hanson, Joseph Mills, b. 1876. Report on the employment of the artillery at the Battle of Antietam, Maryland.
III. Title. IV. Series: Texas A & M University military
history series ; 36.
E474.65.J64 1995
973.7'336—dc20   94-13226
                                                         CIP

Contents

Contents

Illustrations

Foreword
"Artillery Hell": Antietam and Its Cannon
Edwin C. Bearss

My first visit to the Antietam battlefield was in the winter of 1949–50. I then owned my first car and had an interest in the Civil War that had been whetted when I was a boy back in Montana and my father read to me John Thomason's *Jeb Stuart*.

At that time Antietam, as it had been since 1890, was a national battlefield site. As such, it was a second-class park, with a small land base. Interpretation was low-key, consisting of iron tablets placed by the War Department in the 1890s describing battle actions; monuments in stone, including the huge Union soldier known as "Big Simon" in the National Cemetery; and six cannon tubes, their muzzles thrust into the ground, serving as mortuary markers to identify where that number of generals were killed or received their mortal wounds. There were paved park roads and a stone observation tower, built by the three-man commission established by Congress to oversee development of the site; the National Cemetery and the historic public road network; three of the four stone bridges, including the Burnside Bridge, present in 1862; and a small office and museum in the Paul Pelz–designed cemetery lodge. Adjacent to the park and public roads were fields, orchards and woodlots, farmhouses, outbuildings, and fences constituting one of rural America's most pleasing landscapes. West of the National Cemetery was the town of Sharpsburg, little changed, except for amenities dictated by the mid-twentieth century, from its appearance on that day nine decades before when the landscape thereabouts turned red.

Although I did not appreciate it in 1950, Antietam National Battlefield Site lacked an important and popular interpretive feature common to the four national military parks authorized by Congress and established in the 1890s. Unlike at Gettysburg, Chickamauga and Chattanooga, Shiloh, and Vicksburg, at Antietam few if any cannon were unlimbered about the field. This was strange because of the important role played by the "long arm," particularly that of Gen. Robert E. Lee, in the battle.

My first official visit to Antietam came in May, 1961, five years after I had entered on duty with the National Park Service. Two weeks were spent at the park in conjunction with a research assignment that called for a detailed study of troop movements and the development of a historical base map documenting the physical and cultural features of the battlefield, circa 1862. While there I walked the area and reviewed the park files. My strolls revealed a major and significant improvement in interpretation. Scattered at key points about the battlefield were forty-one cannon, far less than at the other War Department parks, but a giant leap forward in enhancing the visitor's appreciation of a battle known as "artillery hell." The cannon—secured through transfer from other parks and agencies or purchase—had been positioned near park and public roads on public lands by the superintendent in the mid-1950s.

I found in the park files a copy of Maj. Joseph Mills Hanson's report "On the Employment of the Artillery at the Battle of Antietam. . . ." Although Major Hanson was dead, his name and work commanded respect, and his report, dog-eared and faded from use, was invaluable to me in my 1961 research efforts.

Since the early 1970s, but particularly since 1977, when I began giving battlefield tours for the Smithsonian Institution's popular Resident Associates Program, I have spent hundreds of hours at Antietam leading tours. Whether it is Antietam, Gettysburg, another Civil War battlefield, or a Revolutionary War winter encampment or battlefield, cannon command attention, whether the participants are the military, buffs, or those with only a casual interest in the Civil and Revolutionary wars. The presence of limbers and caisson enhances the exhibit.

In the spring of 1985, Secretary of the Army John Marsh reinstituted staff rides as an important element of the army's training. To emphasize his interest and support, he asked me to lead a staff ride at Antietam. Participants in the May 4 staff ride, in addition to Secretary Marsh, Assistant Secretary James Ambrose, Chief of Staff John A. Wickham, and Vice Chief of Staff Maxwell Thurmond, were the Army General Staff and a large number of strap-hangers and public affairs officials. Following the ride, we assembled for an outdoor lunch under the trees between the Hagerstown pike and the Maryland monument. Nearby were cannon, limbers, and caisson representing Col. Stephen D. Lee's Confederate Artillery Battalion.

In my critique, I described the vital role played by the Confederate artillery in enabling General Lee to hold his position against repeated Union attacks. I spoke of the need for better-educated and -motivated junior officers and enlisted men in the "long arm" and the long hours on the drill field needed to perfect the necessary skills. When I finished, General Thurmond and several other senior officers stood and applauded and announced that they had entered the army as gunners. General Wickham, holder of the Combat Infantryman Badge and a number of decorations for gallantry, including the Purple Heart, got up and declared that he was an infantryman and that I had shot myself in the foot.

The interest park visitors have in artillery—its guns, equipment, personnel, mission, and role in Civil War combat—along with an appreciation of the significance of the Battle of Antietam and its aftermath have been recognized by Curt Johnson and Richard Anderson, Jr. This interest led to the present publication, with which I am proud to be associated. *Artillery Hell* is an invaluable contribution to our understanding of Civil War field artillery, its weaponry, and its deployment and use at Antietam. It also clarifies the rationale of the National Park Service in the mid-twentieth century governing the positioning of the limited number of cannon to best interpret their key role in the battle.

Included in *Artillery Hell* are a series of essays and compilations by Johnson and Anderson. Curt Johnson, whose bibliography demonstrates a broad interest and understanding of military history from the Thirty Years' War to the Gulf War, leads off with an overview of organizational problems confronting the senior artillerists on the eve of a great battle. The technological revolution in weaponry resulting in the rifle-musket becoming the standard firearm of the infantry compelled artillerists to rethink and revise the tactics that, during the Napoleonic wars, had made the "long arm" the Queen of Battles. In the Mexican War, these tactics had given the United States troops a decisive edge over the Mexican Army from the opening battle of Palo Alto through the capture of Mexico City.

Richard Anderson's contribution on Civil War artillery is masterful. Only once before in nearly forty years as a serious student of the Civil War have I read an essay that so clearly and concisely provides information needed by a battlefield stomper to identify and understand the different types of field artillery and their capabilities—both rifled and smoothbore—and the ammunition employed, with the differences explained in terms familiar to the layman. This basic information is followed by sections focusing on battery organization and tactics, subjects that too many writers fail to understand or explain to their readers.

The core of *Artillery Hell* is Maj. Joseph Mills Hanson's previously referenced 1940 report on the employment of artillery at Antietam. The study was prepared by Major Hanson in response to recognition by senior National Park Service managers that Antietam, unlike the other four 1890s War Department parks, did not have battlefield cannon. Needed cannon would have to be acquired by transfer from other parks or alternative sources.

Hanson, to accomplish his purpose, separated the subject matter into five sections, three of which are included in *Artillery Hell*. They are:

I. Compilations of the batteries in the respective armies at Antietam, showing, so far as the information is available, the designation of each battery, the name of its commander, the number and types of guns that it contained, and the higher unit to which it was attached.

II. A review of the battle actions of the "individual batteries." In doing so, Hanson endeavored successfully to demonstrate "briefly the tactical effects upon the battle produced by the several batteries in their various positions."

III. "A list of battery positions in a tentative order of priority based upon the discussions in Section II." This list was prepared as the bottom line for "a suggested sequence of battery positions to be marked as guns for the purpose become available."

The Hanson report, unlike many government studies, was not filed and forgotten. Since 1940, when Antietam acquired its first eighteen cannon and carriages from Gettysburg National Military Park, the Hanson report has guided the park staff in its selection of what battery positions would be identified and interpreted with Civil War cannon. At present, there are forty-one cannon on the Antietam battlefield, and, except where the appropriate land is not owned by the United States, the Hanson priorities have been observed. This, in view of a desire on the part of new superintendents to make changes for change's sake, underscores the value and the enduring legacy of the Hanson report.

Historians Johnson and Anderson, employing their knowledge, research, and writing skills, build on the Hanson report with chapters on the Union and Confederate artillery at Antietam. Using a number of sources either unavailable to or untapped by Major Hanson and other researchers, principally the Henry Jackson Hunt Papers at the Library of Congress, they have compiled in one publication the answers to most if not all questions that confound and challenge the historian, journalist, and battlefield tourist. Equally important, this basic information on the artillery at Antietam is presented in a form both well-organized and easily understood. Johnson and Anderson have done much to enrich our appreciation of the "long arm" at Antietam. As a thirty-eight-year Park Service employee who has been walking battlefields even longer, I hope that the authors or other readers will be inspired to do the same for Antietam's four sister War Department parks.

As a bonus, the authors have included the after-action reports submitted by six Union battery commanders and found in the Hunt Papers. Only one of these reports was included by the compilers in the *Official Records* of the Union and Confederate armies. Last, but in no way least, the publisher is applauded for including a number of photographs and maps of the present-day battlefield and the Antietam cannon. Too often, because of added costs, these necessary adjuncts to a truly useful publication are slighted.

Joseph Mills Hanson, the only child of Joseph Randall and Annie Marie Gertrude Mills Hanson, was born in Yankton, Dakota Territory, on July 20, 1876, less than four weeks after Lt. Col. George Armstrong Custer and five troops of the 7th U.S. Cavalry were annihilated on the Little Bighorn by Sioux and Cheyenne warriors. The New Hampshire–born father had arrived in the area in 1858 and the following year staked out a land claim on the Missouri River, in what was then Nebraska Territory. Dakota territory was organized in 1861 with Yankton as the seat of government, and Hanson became the territory's first legislative clerk. Subsequently he served as territorial auditor, judge-advocate, and Indian agent. As evidence of his importance in territorial affairs, Hanson County, formed in 1880, was named in his honor. Indicative of his broad interests was his role as a contractor when the Dakota Southern Railroad extended its tracks from Sioux City, Iowa, to Yankton in 1873.

In 1875, Hanson married Annie Mills, a New York City native and graduate of the New England Conservatory of Music, who for health reasons had moved to Dakota Territory. The next year Joseph Mills was born, and from 1879 until he was twelve he lived with his parents in a two-story brick house known as Prospect Place, on Yankton's Rudolph Hill.

Young Joseph attended grammar school in Yankton, and in 1888, two years before South Dakota became a state, his parents sent him east to Boston, where he attended Chauncy Hall School. Upon graduating from the eastern boarding school, Joseph matirculated in the Preparatory Department at Yankton College, then headed back east to attend Saint John's Military School at Manlius, New York, where he graduated in 1890.

His mother's brother was a senior officer in the Otis Elevator Company, and Joseph went to work as a salesman in the company's Saint Louis office. He left Otis in 1909, deciding that he could not find fulfillment in the business world. In that year, A. C. McClurg and Company of Chicago published Hanson's first book, *The Conquest of the Missouri*. He celebrated its release by marrying Frances Lee Johnson of Holden, Missouri, and moving back to Yankton. In 1910, a second book—*The Frontier Ballads*—and a third—*With Sulley into the Sioux Land*—came off the press.

Plagued by ill health, Frances died in 1912. The bereaved widower sought consolation in research and writing. *With Carrington on the Bozeman Trail,* in the year of his wife's death; *The Trail to El Dorado,* in 1913; and *Pilot Knob, the Thermopylae of the West,* in 1914, in collaboration with Cyrus A. Peterson, added to Hanson's bibliography. He wrote a number of articles for local newspapers concerning the early history of Yankton, Dakota Territory, and South Dakota. He also farmed.

With a war raging in Europe and the Middle East, the United States' relations with Mexico further soured. Following a raid on Columbus, New Mexico, by Mexican irregulars led by Pancho Villa, President Woodrow Wilson mobilized a number of National Guard units for service on the border. Among the states called on was South Dakota. Recognizing his military training at Saint John's and his literary interest, Joseph Mills Hanson was commissioned a captain in the South Dakota National Guard on May 1, 1916. As a captain in Company M, 7th South Dakota Infantry, Captain Hanson saw service on the Mexican border from June 21, 1916, to March 9, 1917.

Captain Hanson was back in Yankton only two weeks when he was recalled into federal service. Then, on April 7, the United States declared war on Germany. Captain Hanson and the officers and men of Company M reported for duty at nearby Camp Wildwood. On October 2, the 7th South Dakota Infantry was reorganized and redesignated the 2nd Battalion, 147th Field Artillery, of which Hanson was battalion adjutant.

The battalion sailed from New York for Europe on January 11, 1918. Captain Hanson landed in Liverpool and, after spending some time camped Winnell Down, crossed the English Channel from Southampton to Le Havre. He was posted to the Field Artillery School at Gondrecourt until March 19, 1918, when he was detached from the 147th Field Artillery. He was then ordered to duty at General Headquarters, American Expeditionary Forces (AEF) as officer in charge of Historical Subsection. He retained this assignment until October. At this time Captain Hanson became senior conducting officer for the Visitors' Bureau. From then until November 20, he repeatedly visited the battlefields of Saint Michel and the Meuse-Argonne as an escort for VIPs to the American armies, including the Gompers Labor Mission, Sen. Carter Glass (Virginia), and M. Deschamps of the Paris daily *Temps.*

From November 20, 1918, to June 13, 1919, he was a feature correspondent for *The Stars and Stripes,* the AEF's official newspaper. His contribution was "The Stars and Stripes History of the American Combat Divisions," which appeared serially until the newspaper ceased publication. While on this assignment, Hanson, accompanied by Capt. J. André Smith, the AEF's official artist, toured the western front battlefields from Ypres and the Menin Road, near the English Channel, to the Somme. While detailed to *The Stars and Stripes,* he attended and reported on the organization convention of the American Legion in Paris.

From June 15 to July 15, 1919, he edited the *Report of the Inspector General on the Conduct of the Welfare Societies.* He was present in the Hall of Mirrors on June 28 when the Treaty of Versailles was signed and witnessed the July 14 victory parade. On October 10, 1919, Hanson departed Brest aboard the *America,* and following his return to the United States, he was mustered out of the Army at Camp Dix, New Jersey, on October 30.

Hanson spent the winter of 1919–20 in Washington, D.C. at Army Headquarters preparing a report for the home front on America's part in the Great War. On February 20, 1920, he was commissioned a major in the Field Artillery Reserve and returned to Yankton.

Drawing on what he had seen while in France, Major Hanson continued his literary endeavors in the postwar years. Nineteen hundred and twenty-two saw publication of *The Marne, Historic and Picturesque,* illustrated with fifty drawings by Captain J. André Smith; "America's Battles in the Great War," published serially in *The Independent: The Stereoscopic History of the World War,* published by Keystone View Company (1922–23); *The World War through the Stereoscope* (1926); and numerous articles on American fighting men in *The American Legion Weekly.*

In 1926 Major Hanson remarried. His second wife was Rosamond Brightman Wellington of Swansea, Massachusetts, a member of the board of the Yankton College endowment campaign. The couple lived in Prospect Place, which the major had inherited on the death of his parents. Writing and farming kept him busy until 1930, when the worsening agricultural depression caused him to abandon his efforts to operate the farm as a supplement to his income from his literary work. Hanson and his wife left the Yankton area to reside in the East.

On August 10, 1933, the National Park Service of the Department of the Interior assumed responsibility under executive order for administering a number of national military parks, national cemeteries, and all national monuments formerly overseen by the War and Agriculture departments. Until this time, the National Park Service's energy and attention had been focused on the West and its great natural wonderland parks. In 1931, following the establishment of Colonial National Monument and confronted by the sesquicentennial of the Battle of Yorktown, the Park Service hired three professional historians, two posted at Colonial and one, Chief Historian Verne Chatelain, in the Washington office. The 1933 reorganization came at an opportune time, coincident with the

inauguration of Franklin D. Roosevelt's New Deal and its emerging
conservation programs. Now, with responsibility for developing the newer
military parks and upgrading interpretation at all of them, including the
five established before 1900, the door was opened for a rapid expansion
of the Service's history program.

By the winter of 1933–34, Chief Historian Chatelain had a staff of
historians larger than that of any major university. Among those hired
was Major Hanson. Like most of the new employees, Hanson was assigned to the Washington headquarters, where he and a number of his
colleagues were allotted office space at the Library of Congress. Other
newly employed historians took up duty stations at the parks.

Major Hanson, during his years as a staff historian, undertook a
number of special studies to support development and interpretive programs at three recently established parks: Appomattox Courthouse National Historical Monument (1930), Richmond National Battlefield Park
(1936), and Saratoga National Historical Park (1938). He also was assigned to prepare a project at Antietam. Unlike its sister War Department
parks dating to the 1890s—Chickamauga and Chattanooga, Shiloh, Gettysburg, and Vicksburg—Antietam was a battlefield with limited acre-
age, no interpretation beyond the iron War Department tablets, and no
battlefield cannon. Senior park service management recognized the need
to upgrade interpretation at Antietam, and cognizant of the popularity of
cannon among visitors to the Civil War parks, they gave Major Hanson
the challenging task of preparing a report on artillery at Antietam. Such
a task was welcomed by the old artillerist.

Major Hanson's report, submitted as a typescript on February 14,
1940, and an essential component of this publication, is entitled "A
Report on the Employment of the Artillery at the Battle of Antietam,
Maryland, with a View to Marking Battery Positions at the Antietam
National Battlefield Site."

By June, 1940, emergency conservation funds had been cut back by
the administration and Congress. In the weeks following the miracle of
Dunkirk and the fall of France, America looked to its defenses and to
giving all aid to Britain and her allies short of war. The corps of research
historians assigned to the Washington office was broken up, and those
retained by the National Park Service were sent to the field. Major
Hanson had a jump-start on this reallocation of resources when in 1939
he became a historian at Petersburg National Military Park. He held this
position until March 31, 1942, when he reported for duty as custodian of
Manassas National Battlefield Park. The park was less than two years
old, having been established in May, 1940. With the United States at war,
Park Service appropriations were slashed and little effort was made to fill

positions left vacant by personnel joining the military or seeking employment in defense industries. Visitation plummeted in the face of wartime fuel rationing. Major Hanson made the best of a grim situation. The park remained open, and he focused his attention on development of a first-class museum in the newly completed Henry Hill visitor center. In the months following V-J Day and the end of rationing, the major continued to serve the public as America again took to the road. Although he celebrated his seventieth birthday in July, 1946, and had reached the mandatory Civil Service retirement age, Hanson twice secured waivers.

Not until December 31, 1947, did he close his productive 14-year National Park Service career. His retirement party, attended by a number of friends, was held at the park visitor center on December 20. In recognition of his work as historian and Park Service manager, Garret Jex, a well-known local artist, painted a portrait of Major Hanson that has since hung in the Manassas visitor center.

The major remained active during his retirement years. He wrote *Bull Run Remembers: The History, Traditions, and Landmarks of the Manassas (Bull Run) Campaigns before Washington, 1861–1862,* published in 1951. Forty years later, in 1991, the Prince William County Historical Commission, recognizing that the first edition had become a collector's item, came out with a second edition, "to stimulate an interest in the local Civil War history."

On February 11, 1960, Major Hanson died, and his body was returned by his wife to his native Yankton for burial.

Preface

Full details of the strength, organization, and tactical employment of the field artillery of the opposing armies at the Battle of Antietam (Sharpsburg, Maryland, September 17, 1862) are not fully known, although the role of artillery in the battle was of decisive importance—to an extent greater than in most Civil War battles.

Another persistent problem has been the question of just how the opposing artilleries were organized, particularly because both were struggling to reorganize and reequip and, at the same time, overcome the debilitating effects of a summer of hard campaigning.

The effects of this reorganization, including rationalized command and control, were manifest in the tactical employment of the artillery on both sides. At Antietam, however, for a variety of reasons, there were breakdowns and expedient reversions to earlier practice. These have often been overlooked or minimized by analysts generally (and uncritically) impresssed by the remarkable achievements of the artillery during the battle.

The Hanson report, reprinted in its entirety here, is a useful antidote to many of the misconceptions about the strength, organization, and tactical employment of the artillery at Antietam. Prepared in 1940 by National Park Service historian Joseph Mills Hanson, it was a pioneering effort to establish the facts surrounding the use of artillery at Antietam. In some respects it has been superseded, but in many others it remains valid: an interesting, informative, and valuable contribution to Civil War scholarship that has not previously been available generally.

To complement Hanson's report, we have provided the fruits of our own labors on this research problem. Because we used some sources not available or accessible to Hanson and other researchers, it is expected that our efforts have added to the fund of knowledge about the battle remembered by many as "Artillery Hell."

Some of the documentation we used, including after-action reports and related documents of the Army of the Potomac, is here printed for the first time. These records were found in the Henry Jackson Hunt

Papers at the Library of Congress and, apparently, were not available to the editors of the *Official Records.*

In addition, we have provided brief notes and descriptions of organization, tactics, and matériel of the field artillery of the American Civil War.

We gratefully acknowledge the generous assistance of professional historians and archivists of the federal government at many junctures. In particular: Ted Alexander and Paul Chiles at Antietam National Battlefield; David Nathanson and his staff at the Harpers Ferry Center of the National Park Service; Ed Raus at Manassas National Battlefield Park; and Robert K. Krick of the Fredericksburg and Spotsylvania National Military Park. Thanks are due as well to the staffs of the National Archives and the Library of Congress, Washington, D.C. (particularly those of the Manuscript Division and the Local History and Geneaology Reading Room).

Special mention must be made of the gracious hospitality and knowledgeable assistance afforded to us by John Ingalls and Katharine L. Crane of the Jefferson County (West Virginia) Museum, depository of the Roger Preston Chew Papers. This small museum, located in Charles Town, is a treasure trove of artifacts relating to the John Brown raid and trial and, of course, the Civil War.

The photographs of the battlefield were taken at the direction of a somewhat demanding (but indulgent) father by Stephanie Johnson in October, 1991, and developed by Pascal Météyer Photographe of Paris, France, in 1992. Maps and related artwork are the product of the genius of A. D. "Durf" McJoynt, our longtime colleague and friend.

We would also like to express our gratitude to Edwin C. Bearss, chief historian of the National Park Service and one of the deans of Civil War scholarship. When asked to write the foreword to this book and, especially, to describe the work of Joseph Mills Hanson from the perspective of a colleague and scholar, Mr. Bearss most generously and without hesitation agreed.

It remains to be said that if any errors have crept into the present work, they are our responsibility alone.

Artillery Hell

1

Introduction
The Operational-Tactical Situation
Curt Johnson

The Second Bull Run (Second Manassas) and Maryland campaigns of August–September, 1862, constituted a fast-moving operational situation, with major combats or battles on a frequent basis. From August 16, when the Second Bull Run campaign began, until September 20, when the Maryland campaign ended, units and formations were marching and fighting—under appalling conditions—almost continuously. The strength of the armies was sapped not only by battle casualties, sickness, and disease but also by straggling, which in September assumed enormous proportions.

For the opposing artilleries, which consisted not only of men but also of horseflesh and all manner of matériel, the campaigns of midsummer and the earlier peninsular and Shenandoah Valley battles had been arduous, debilitating experiences. As much as the opposing infantry and cavalry had been weakened by attrition, the artillery had suffered even further, since its losses were more difficult to replace.

Robert E. Lee's Army of Northern Virginia numbered approximately 40,000 men when it crossed the Potomac into Maryland during September 4–7, 1862. The exact number is not known, but the army's strength was much reduced from the 50,000 that had fought and won the Second Bull Run campaign. This was true despite a large reinforcement (divisions of D. H. Hill, McLaws, and Walker, plus Hampton's cavalry brigade: about 22,000 men in all) that more than offset the 9,000 casualties incurred in the campaign just concluded.

Straggling was the critical problem, particularly in an army in which most of the men were shoeless, filthy, ragged, and starving (the countryside in northern Virginia was a literal wasteland). In this instance, however, it was compounded by the fact that multitudes of Confederates were opposed on political grounds to invading the North, and they "voted with their feet" by joining the shoeless hordes herded into the Upper Valley by the provost guard. Truly, as historian David Donald has stated, the epi-

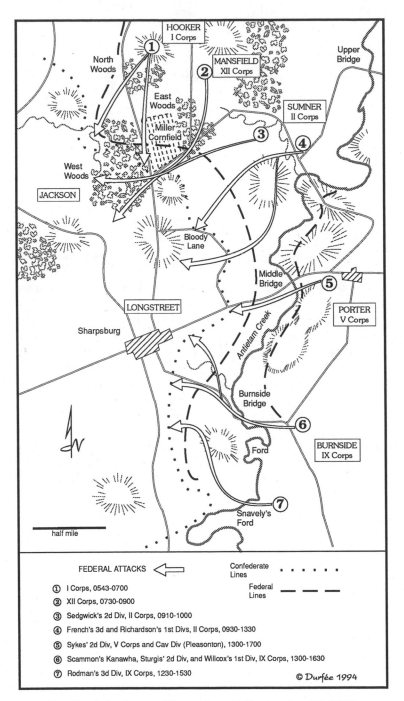

FEDERAL ATTACKS ⟵   Confederate
                        Lines · · · · · ·

① I Corps, 0543-0700   Federal
                              Lines – – –
② XII Corps, 0730-0900

③ Sedgwick's 2d Div, II Corps, 0910-1000

④ French's 3d and Richardson's 1st Divs, II Corps, 0930-1330

⑤ Sykes' 2d Div, V Corps and Cav Div (Pleasonton), 1300-1700

⑥ Scammon's Kanawha, Sturgis' 2d Div, and Willcox's 1st Div, IX Corps, 1300-1630

⑦ Rodman's 3d Div, IX Corps, 1230-1530

© Durfée 1994

Battle of Antietam (Sharpsburg), September 17, 1862

taph on the Confederacy's tombstone should have read "Died of Democracy."

The Confederate artillery was in the midst of a reorganization, and on paper at least had largely achieved the ideal of having one artillery battalion per division for direct support, with one battalion per corps (wing) and the general reserve of the army for general support. To a limited extent, this organization was effective by the time of Antietam, and, indeed, it had first shown its potential at Second Manassas. Its effectiveness, however, was limited by the heavy hand of tradition and by the limited capabilities of certain field officers.

The reorganization was more complete in Jackson's corps than it was in Longstreet's. As late as August 18, 1862, while Longstreet's corps was organizing for the Second Manassas campaign, eleven batteries in hand were assigned as follows: nine for direct support of infantry brigades and two for the general reserve. "The several captains were ordered to report immediately to the brigade commanders for duty during the present campaign" (Owen 1885, p. 100).

The Washington Artillery of New Orleans (four companies), which might have constituted a battalion for field service, was divided: its 2nd and 4th companies were assigned to Pickett's and Toombs's brigades, respectively; and its 1st and 3rd companies formed the corps reserve. The organization adopted by Longstreet's wing at this time was preserved through the Sharpsburg campaign, although not all the batteries assigned to brigades were at Sharpsburg, and several were broken up in October.

Complicating problems of reorganization were endemic shortages of matériel. Although the artillery that had fought the Second Bull Run campaign was augmented by a mass of guns (thirty-one batteries) that came up from Richmond after Second Bull Run, only efficient batteries were allowed to cross into Maryland. Many inefficient, broken-down units had to be left behind.

Another problem of the Confederate artillery at this time was the heterogeneity of the matériel in the batteries. Of the fifty-nine batteries present at Antietam, only five had a uniform armament. Batteries with three or even four different types of guns were not unusual. It may be that no modern field armies exhibited such an assortment of matériel as did those of the Confederacy at this time. Besides complicating ammunition supply and resupply, this situation made the job of the battery commander almost nightmarish and limited the real combat potential of most batteries in common battlefield circumstances. Very often only rifled pieces or sections—when available—could be employed against the uniformly more modern, heavier, and longer-ranging Federal artillery.

Compounding the situation was the obsolescence of much of the

matériel. The Army of the Potomac was armed with guns that were
entirely modern and equivalent to the best matériel in service in the
world. The few Mexican War pieces in the Federal army's inventory
were heavy guns that were not out of place on the modern battlefield. By
contrast, the Army of Northern Virginia fielded a large number of Mexican War–vintage M-1841 6-lb. guns, reliable and efficient pieces but
sorely inferior in both hitting power and range to the more modern
weapons of their opponents. Whenever possible, these antique pieces
were replaced by captured or imported guns.

When Maj. Gen. George B. McClellan assumed command of the
Army of the Potomac in early September, he appointed Col. Henry J.
Hunt the army's chief of artillery, replacing Brig. Gen. William F. Barry,
who became chief of artillery of the defenses of Washington. Hunt, who
had previously commanded the army's Artillery Reserve, inherited a
position that had been largely nominal. Lacking a staff and (to a degree)
real authority, he set about reorganizing the army's artillery arm, which
he found in deplorable condition. Besides longstanding problems of
organization, many batteries were deficient in men, horses, and guns (or
other matériel) and consequently were inefficient.

Most of the problems of the artillery stemmed from McClellan's
peninsula campaign or Maj. Gen. John Pope's recently concluded maneuvers in northern Virginia. The loss of matériel in both campaigns had
been great (the Confederates captured thirty guns at Second Bull Run
alone), and Hunt's most immediate problem was to reequip the army's
artillery. This he largely accomplished in a very short time. Moreover, by
combing the baggage trains for horses and the infantry for men, he was
able to relieve much of the deficiency in those areas.

Initially, the organizational problem was overlooked or honored more
in the breach. Hooker's I Corps went into combat at Antietam with the
same decentralized organization that had obtained on the peninsula, and
the army's Artillery Reserve was but a shadow of its former potent self.
On the other hand, centralization of command and control functions and
the assignment of the regular batteries to formations in the proportion of
one regular to three volunteer batteries was proceeding under difficult
circumstances.

The very fact that Hunt attempted immediately to sort things out in
the chaos of defeat and in the midst of large strategic movements and
fundamental reorganizations and recorded his efforts has permitted us to
definitively transcribe the artillery organization of the Army of the Potomac at Antietam. Hunt's papers, on deposit at the Library of Congress,
were the key to answering many of the questions on this subject that have
persisted until this day.

Another problem Hunt tackled, and continued to address even with the battle in progress, was the bad tactical habits of many of his gunners. In particular, they had a penchant for rapid, indiscriminate firing and the related practice of withdrawing the guns after the ready ammunition had been fired off. (The same phenomenon was noted in the Prussian artillery during the Seven Weeks' War in 1866.) Charles Cuffel of Durell's battery related that during the Battle of Antietam, Hunt "rode along the line and gave orders to the commanders of batteries to fire slowly and deliberately; stating that rapid firing did little execution and was a waste of ammunition." He added that Hunt, "a small grizzly man with an effeminate voice," but withal "an experienced and able artillerist," was obeyed (Cuffel 1900, p. 78).

When finally the armies faced one another at Antietam, they were much reduced in strength. On the other hand, those who went into combat at daybreak on September 17 were for the most part the elite of two very good armies: physically tough, hard-bitten veterans led by experienced officers who well understood the realities of mid-nineteenth–century combat and what was at stake. This fact goes far to explain the unparalleled murderous intensity of America's "bloodiest day."

Much of the fighting was stubborn; occasionally, it was severe in the extreme. The artillery combat, however, was particularly prolonged and intense, and it may be that Lee's army owed its salvation to the sacrificial valor of its much outnumbered guns and devoted gunners. It is not surprising, then, that one of those gunners should have described Antietam as "artillery hell" (Wise 1959, p. 323), while the artillery's historian characterized it as "a day of glory for the Confederate artillery" (Wise 1959).

On the Union side, the artillery's achievement was no less remarkable. Having been, in Hunt's words, "organized on the march and in the intervals of conflict," it performed to a high standard and admirably supported the various uncoordinated attacks of the Federal infantry. Whether firing at long range from the hills east of the Antietam or from positions well forward in Miller's Cornfield and at Bloody Lane and elsewhere on that memorable field, the Union artillery exceeded the reputation that it had gained at Malvern Hill. Its notoriety caused Confederate Maj. Gen. Daniel Harvey Hill to remark, "Confederate infantry and Federal artillery, side by side on the same field, need fear no foe on earth" (Johnson and Buell 1956, 2:395).

View north from S. D. Lee's first position toward the Smoketown Road and the cornfield, showing four of the various types of field artillery weapons employed at Antietam. *From left:* 3-in. Ordnance rifle (wrought iron); 10-lb. Parrott rifle; 12-lb. Napoleon gun–howitzer; and Model 1841, Mexican War–vintage 6-lb. gun.

View north from S. D. Lee's first position toward Miller's Cornfield and the East Woods. The latter were more extensive in 1862. The view looks over Mumma's plowed field, where Woolfolk's section under Lt. William D. Terrell lost two guns opposing the advance of Tyndale's Brigade.

View north by northwest from the Indiana monument, looking down the
Hagerstown pike from the south border of the cornfield toward the Miller
farm *(middle ground)*. This was the scene of the savage struggle between
Campbell's Battery B, 4th U.S., and the left-flank elements of Wofford's
Brigade—the 4th Texas, Hampton Legion, and the 18th Georgia—at ca.
0720. Campbell's Battery was in position on the left (west) side of the pike
in the foreground. The Hampton Legion infantry faced Campbell from the
vantage point.

View east across Miller's Cornfield toward the west fringe of the East Woods, about 350 yards distant. The terrain shown was the scene of much intense fighting during the battle's morning phase. During the forenoon Frank's Battery G (1st New York) and Vanneman's Battery B (Maryland Light) were in position opposite the viewer. By noon these batteries had been integrated into a line of guns and supporting infantry established by the VI Corps to cover the gap between Sumner's left at Bloody Lane and his shattered right, which had been driven northward *(left)* after its repulse from the West Woods.

Nicodemus Heights viewed from the Union I Corps position in the North Woods—Poffenberger Lane sector. In 1862 the woods extended to the Hagerstown pike *(foreground)*. A powerful concentration of Union guns on open ground north *(right)* of the vantage point protected Hooker's refused right flank, while Pelham's group of guns on Nicodemus Heights raked the Miller farm south *(left)* of the vantage point and defended Lee's left.

View west-southwest across the cornfield from the west fringe of the East Woods toward the West Woods. This was the approximate position during the morning of Matthews's Battery F, 1st Pennsylvania Light (ca. 0800 hrs.); and Bruen's 10th Battery, New York Light (ca. 1000). During the mid- to late afternoon Hazard's Battery B (1st Rhode Island) and Frank's Battery G (1st New York) were positioned here. Thompson's Independent Battery C (Pennsylvania Light) was in position about midway across the cornfield and firing south *(left)* at ca. 0900 hrs.

The column in the distance surmounted by an officer waving a sword is the New Jersey monument at the Hagerstown pike, marking the approximate position of the rookie 13th New Jersey when it was stopped by deadly fire from Confederates of Early's Brigade. Early's men seemed to rise from the ground in their front and were in fact sheltered by a limestone shelf that formed a natural trench facing the pike (shelf visible from Starke Avenue today).

View east-northeast toward the southern extremity of the East Woods and Mumma's farm, with the Smoketown Road crossing the field of view diagonally from left to right center. The Dunkard Church is to the rear of the viewer. From ca. 0800 to 1000 hrs. Monroe's Battery D (1st Rhode Island) was positioned on the rising ground about midway up the road on the right (south) side. Tompkins's Battery A (1st Rhode Island) was on Monroe's left, out of the photo to the right. Knap's Independent Battery B (Pennsylvania Light) was on the left of the road.

View east-northeast from the Hagerstown pike west of Piper's house and barn toward Graham's (Battery K, 1st U.S.) position at Bloody Lane (observation tower, *right*), distant about 900 yards. At about 1300 hrs. the area in the foreground and to the right was occupied by batteries of Saunders's Battalion (R. H. Anderson's Division). The opposing guns were engaged in a fierce struggle for dominance of the intervening terrain. Miller's 3rd Company, Washington Artillery, was in battery in the middle ground, approximately, and may have been the battery driven off by Graham's fire.

The rocky field in the foreground was the scene of the ill-fated attack of the 7th Maine (Irwin's Brigade) in the late afternoon. Gunfire from the Union batteries of Williston, Hexamer, and Woodruff swept Piper's orchard *(middle distance)* to protect the withdrawal of the Maine infantry (see Williston's AAR, printed here for the first time).

View west-southwest toward the Piper farm (white buildings, 750 yards distant, *left center*) from Graham's position at Bloody Lane. Confederate batteries in the Piper cornfield *(middle distance)* and on the high ground beyond the Hagerstown pike (1,400 yards distant) dueled with Graham and eventually caused him to retire, his battery cut to pieces.

\

Close-up view of Piper's barn, looking west-southwest from the observation
tower above Graham's position at Bloody Lane. Piper's cornfield (Miller's
position) is in the middle ground. Grimes's and Maurin's batteries of Saunders's Battalion were in position near the barn (Grimes KIA there), along
with Carter's Battery of Pierson's Battalion. The high ground at the tree line
beyond the barn was crowned by other batteries—Peyton's (H. P. Jones's
Battalion), Macon's (Cabell's Battalion), and Hardaway's (Pierson's Battalion), among others. Hardaway's rifles may have been the guns that caused
Graham so much trouble.

View east-southeast toward the Branch monument from the position of Pegram's Battery (Walker's Battalion) overlooking the ground crossed *(right to left)* by Gregg's and Branch's brigades in A. P. Hill's counterattack that drove in the Union left (Rodman's Division). C. P. Muhlenberg's Battery and other Union guns that had come forward from Burnside Bridge were in position along the tree line on the distant ridge but were neutralized by Confederate guns here and to the right and right front. Elk Ridge (Union signal station) is on the horizon.

View east-southeast toward the J. Otto house from the position of Confederate batteries on Cemetery Hill (Moody's, Garden's, Maurin's, and Squires's,
among others) overlooking ground crossed by Willcox's Division in its
attack on Sharpsburg. Here, Welsh's brigade attacked directly toward the
viewer against the Confederate brigades of Drayton *(right)* and Jenkins
(left). Union batteries in support near the Otto house were Clark's E, 4th
U.S., and Cook's 8th Massachusetts Light. Roemer's Battery may also have
been in position in the vicinity of the Otto house.

2

Civil War Field Artillery
Richard C. Anderson, Jr.

To assist the reader in understanding the formidable—and somewhat bewildering—array of terms and designations in this book, we provide below a synoptic guide to Civil War field artillery matériel, organization, and tactics.

Smoothbore Artillery

The **Model 1857 12-lb. light gun–howitzer (Napoleon)** was developed in France under the auspices of Emperor Napoleon III in 1856. The U.S. Army Ordnance Department obtained a license to produce the gun in 1857.

With a propellant charge of 2.50 lbs. of black powder, the Napoleon fired a 12.30-lb. solid shot to a range of 1,619 yards at five degrees elevation. The muzzle velocity was 1,485 feet per second (f.p.s.). Ammunition types included solid shot, spherical case, common shell, and canister. The tube was made of bronze (commonly, and incorrectly, known as brass). It was 66 inches long and weighed 1,227 lbs. The carriage weighed 1,128 lbs. for a total combat weight of 2,355 lbs. The bore had a diameter of 4.62 inches.

The Napoleon was the favorite field gun of both armies. It was reasonably accurate at all ranges and was devastating when firing canister at close range. The Napoleon was robustly designed (in modern parlance it was "overengineered") and was capable of firing large numbers of rounds (more than 1,200 rounds for a six-gun battery in a single engagement was not uncommon) without any noticeable distortion or wear on the tube. In one incident at Antietam, an inexperienced infantryman of the Iron Brigade helped man a gun of Campbell's Battery (B, 4th U.S.) in the repulse of Hood's attack. The infantryman blithely loaded double canister and fired away—unaware that he was supposed to remove the powder charge for the second round before loading! The overcharged gun bucked violently into the air with each round, but it was found to be fully serviceable at the end of the battle.

The **Model 1841 6-lb. gun** was one of a "family" of weapons designed by the U.S. Army Ordnance Department in 1841 (companion pieces were the Model 1841 12-lb., 24-lb., and 32-lb. howitzers; the Model 1841 12-lb. gun; and the Model 1841 12-lb. mountain howitzer). The effectiveness of the 1841 series was proven in the Mexican War, during which U.S. ordnance gained an outstanding reputation for maneuverability and reliability.

With a propellant charge of 1.25 lbs., the 6-lb. gun fired a 6.10-lb. solid shot to a range of 1,523 yards at five degrees elevation. The muzzle velocity was 1,450 f.p.s. Ammunition types included solid shot, spherical case, common shell, and canister. Like the Napoleon, the tube of the 6-lb. gun was made of bronze and weighed 884 lbs. (A pattern with an iron tube—cheaper, but heavier and more brittle—existed and was common in Confederate manufacture.) The carriage weighed 900 lbs. for a total combat weight of 1,784 lbs. The diameter of the bore was 3.67 inches, while the length of the tube was 60 inches.

The 6-lb. gun was common to both armies in the early war years. The piece gradually fell into disfavor, however, because of its limited hitting power (the smaller bore diameter made it less effective than the Napoleon when firing canister). Some 6-lb. guns were converted to rifled muzzleloaders (usually of the James pattern, as discussed below), but many of the remainder were melted down and recast as Napoleons. In the western armies (both Union and Confederate), however, the 6-lb. gun soldiered on in small numbers until the end of the war.

The **Model 1841 12-lb. howitzer** was the companion piece to the 6-lb. gun in the 1841 Ordnance series. As a howitzer, it was designed to fire at a higher trajectory than guns in order to attack targets masked to flat trajectory fire.

With a 1-lb. propellant charge, the 12-lb. howitzer fired an 8.90-lb. shell to a range of 1,072 yards at five degrees elevation. Ammunition types included spherical case, common shell, and canister. The bronze tube weighed 788 lbs. and was 53 inches long. (As with the 6-lb. gun, an iron-tube pattern existed but was only common in Confederate service.) The diameter of the bore was 4.62 inches. The carriage weighed 900 lbs. (the same carriage was used for both the 6-lb. gun and the 12-lb. howitzer) for a total combat weight of 1,688 lbs.

The 12-lb. howitzer was an effective, serviceable piece. Its performance was poor, however, compared to the more modern Napoleon. In Federal service it was quickly replaced by the Napoleon except in the western armies, where it was used in small numbers until the end of the war. The Confederate experience was similar: most of their 12-lb. howitzers were eventually recast as Napoleons.

The **Model 1841 12-lb. gun** was the heavy field gun in the 1841 Ordnance series. It was replaced by the lighter and more effective Napoleon and was not commonly found on Civil War battlefields. It is believed that neither the Union nor Confederate armies employed the 12-lb. gun at Sharpsburg; however, a number were captured by Jackson at Harpers Ferry.

The 12-lb. gun used the same propellant charges and types of ammunition as the Napoleon, but its longer tube (78 inches) developed a slightly higher muzzle velocity and thus achieved a range of 1,663 yards at five degrees elevation. The tube, however, weighed 1,757 lbs., 530 lbs. more than the Napoleon. The carriage weighed 1,175 lbs., for a total combat weight of 2,932 lbs., 577 lbs. more than the Napoleon. The diameter of the bore was 4.62 inches, the same as the Napoleon.

The **Model 1841 24-lb. howitzer** was the heaviest ordnance intended for field operations in the 1841 series. With a propellant charge of 2 lbs., the 24-lb. howitzer fired an 18.40-lb. shell to a range of 1,322 yards at five degrees elevation. The ammunition types used were the same as those for the 12-lb. howitzer. The bronze tube weighed 1,318 lbs. and was 65 inches long. The carriage weighed 1,128 lbs., for a total combat weight of 2,446 lbs. The diameter of the bore was 5.82 inches.

The 24-lb. howitzer was not commonly used in the field in Federal service. Its relatively short range and heavy weight made it unpopular. The piece enjoyed some popularity in Confederate service, however, where it was noted for its accuracy and hitting power.

The **Model 1841 32-lb. howitzer** was intended for siege operations, but a few were taken into the field. At Antietam, Battery D of the First New York Light Artillery Battalion was equipped with this piece. (This battalion was the core of McClellan's siege train.)

With a 2.50-lb. propellant charge, the 32-lb. howitzer could fire a 25.60-lb. shell to 1,504 yards at five degrees elevation. Ammunition types were the same as those for the 12-lb. and 24-lb. howitzers. The bronze tube weighed 1,920 lbs. and was 75 inches long. The carriage weighed 1,175 lbs., for a total combat weight of 3,095 lbs. The diameter of the bore was 6.40 inches.

The massive weight of the 32-lb. howitzer made it unpopular for field use. After Antietam, Battery D was reequipped with 3-inch Ordnance rifles.

The **12-lb. (Dahlgren) boat howitzer** was designed for the U.S. Navy for use on ships' boats. A simple wrought-iron carriage was provided for field use, and a rifled version also existed. With a 1-lb. propellant charge, the 12-lb. boat howitzer fired a 10-lb. shell to 1,085 yards at five degrees elevation. Ammunition types were the same as for the army howitzers. The bronze tube weighed 760 lbs. and was 55 inches long. The diameter of the bore was 4.60 inches.

This lightweight piece was used by the 9th New York Volunteer Infantry's Battery Company K and by Grimes's Portsmouth (Virginia) Battery. Although not widely employed, the weapon was evidently popular. When the reduction of personnel in Grimes's battery forced its members to trim their weapons inventory, the battery turned in a 3-inch Ordnance rifle at the start of the campaign instead of one of its naval howitzers.

Rifled Artillery

The **10-lb. Parrott rifled muzzleloader** was one of the two most common rifled fieldpieces used by the Union and Confederate armies. It was designed by Captain Robert P. Parrott before the war. The tube of the Parrott rifle was made of cast iron with a heavy wrought-iron band reinforcing the breech.

With a 1-lb. propellant charge, the 10-lb. Parrott fired a 9.50-lb. solid shot to 1,900 yards with a five-degree elevation. The tube weighed 899 lbs. and was 74 inches long. The bore, originally 2.90 inches, was later changed to 3.00 inches in order to allow commonality of ammunition with the 3-inch Ordnance rifle. The carriage was the same as that for the 6-lb. gun and weighed 900 lbs., for a total combat weight of 1,799 lbs. The 10-lb. Parrott had a good reputation for accuracy and was considered reasonably reliable.

The **3-inch Ordnance rifled muzzleloader** was the second most common rifled field gun found in the Union and Confederate armies. This rifle was manufactured by wrapping wrought-iron sheets around a mandrel. The cylinder formed was heated and welded and was then cooled, bored, turned, and rifled.

With a 1-lb. propellant charge, the 3-inch rifle fired a 9.50-lb. shot to 1,830 yards at five degrees elevation. The tube weighed 820 lbs and was 69 inches long. The carriage was again that of the 6-lb. gun and weighed 900 lbs., for a total combat weight of 1,720 lbs. The diameter of the bore was 3 inches.

The 3-inch Ordnance rifle was probably the most popular fieldpiece of the war. It was accurate and completely reliable in action: there was only a single instance of a 3-inch rifle bursting in action on the Union side during the war. The Confederate Ordnance Department also produced its own version of the 3-inch Ordnance rifle. Low-precision rifle boring machinery and the use of low-grade iron ore, however, made the Confederate guns less reliable. Those produced by the firm of Burton and Archer were notorious, both for their poor accuracy and for their poor reliability.

The **20-lb. Parrott rifle** was the heaviest rifled fieldpiece ordinarily taken into the field. With a propellant charge of 2 lbs., the 20-lb. Parrott fired a 20-lb. shot 1,900 yards at five degrees elevation. The tube weighed 1,750 lbs. and was 84 inches long. The carriage was similar to that of the 12-lb. gun and weighed 1,175 lbs., for a total combat weight of 2,925 lbs. The diameter of the bore was 3.67 inches.

The 20-lb. Parrott was a highly accurate piece. Unfortunately, its reputation for reliability was not good. In common with all Parrott guns, the 20-lb. rifle had the distressing habit of bursting at the breech after prolonged firing. Although not as common an event as with the larger Parrott siege rifles, bursting occurred with enough frequency to make firing a somewhat nerve-wracking affair. Its great weight and unreliability combined to make it an unpopular fieldpiece. After Antietam, most of the 20-lb. Parrott rifles in the Army of the Potomac were replaced by 10-lb. Parrotts and 3-inch Ordnance rifles.

The **12-lb. James rifled muzzleloader** was an early attempt to convert smoothbore guns to rifles. The 12-lb. James was a 6-lb. gun that had been bored out and then fitted with an iron- or brass-rifled liner. Unfortunately, the higher chamber pressures generated in the rifle placed a heavy strain on the breech. James rifles had a notorious habit of bursting in action. Compounding this was the fact that the standard brass liner wore out quickly, markedly reducing accuracy after a few rounds had been fired. Most were withdrawn from service early in the war.

With a 0.75-lb. propellant charge, the 12-lb. James rifle fired a 12-lb. solid shot to 1,700 yards at five degrees elevation. The tube weighed 875 lbs. and was 60 inches long. With the carriage of the 6-lb. gun weighing 900 lbs., the total combat weight was 1,775 lbs. The diameter of the bore was 3.67 inches.

The **12-lb. Blakely rifled muzzleloader** was an imported cast-steel weapon. Like the Parrott, the British-made Blakely had a heavy wrought-iron reinforcing band at the breech. With a 1-lb. propellant charge, the 12-lb. Blakely fired a 10-lb. shot to 1,850 yards at five degrees elevation. The tube weighed 800 lbs. and was 59 inches long. The carriage was again that of the 6-lb. gun—900 lbs.—for a total combat weight of 1,700 lbs. The diameter of the bore was 3.40 inches.

The Blakely appears to have been used only by the Confederate Army and in very small numbers. It was considered to be highly accurate and reliable. It was famous, however, for its massive recoil (probably a consequence of its relatively light weight and short tube). Gunner Neese of Chew's battery described the Blakely as a "vicious little recoiler" (Neese 1911, p. 121), and McHenry Howard, a staff officer, commented that they "kicked like a mule, and for this and other reasons they gradually disappeared" (Howard 1914, p. 168n).

Whitworth rifled muzzleloaders were imported British steel rifles of incredible range and accuracy (for the day). The Whitworth was manufactured as a 6-lb. muzzleloader, a 12-lb. muzzleloader, and a 12-lb. breechloader. The type(s) used by the Confederate batteries known to have had them at Antietam is unknown.

Ammunition

Ammunition for smoothbores was normally "fixed," that is, the projectile and the propellant charge were attached to one another for ease of loading. Ammunition for rifled guns was normally semifixed, with the projectile and propellant charge being loaded separately.

Solid shot and **rifle bolts** were the most common artillery rounds fired. Smoothbore ordnance used the spherical "shot"; rifled ordnance the cylindro-conoidal "bolt." In both types the round was usually made of cast iron. Casualties resulted from the impact of the round upon the target or from the spray of fragments thrown out by the shot hitting the ground.

Common shell was a hollow projectile with a black, powder-filled cavity. Shells fired from smoothbore ordnance were fitted with a time fuze that detonated the shell at various ranges. Shells for rifled ordnance were fitted with either a time fuze or a percussion fuze (placed in the nose of the projectile and detonating upon impact). When correctly fuzed, casualties were caused by the fragmentation of the casing and (occasionally) by the concussive effects of the explosion. Both time and percussion fuzes were temperamental, however. Time fuzes were likely to go off either too late (in which case the intended target could vacate the area or, at least in a few documented cases, a brave soul could put out the fuze) or too early (sometimes with distressing results for friendly troops in the line of fire). Percussion fuzes also had problems. In many cases the delay between projectile impact and fuze ignition was significant. Usually this meant that the round would bury itself in the ground before the explosion, reducing the effect. At other times the round would tumble in flight (Confederate rifle shells manufactured by Burton and

Archer were famous for this). If the tumbling round hit tail first, the percussion cap would not be struck and the round would fail to explode.

Spherical case, a refinement of the common shell, was developed by British General Sir Henry Shrapnel (thus, "shrapnel" shell). In spherical case the black-powder bursting charge was surrounded by a large number of cast-iron balls (for a Napoleon there were seventy-eight balls; for a 6-lb. gun there were thirty-eight). The bursting charge blasted these iron balls in all directions; common shell typically fragmented into a small number of projectiles, limiting its lethality. When correctly fuzed, spherical case could have the same devastating effect as canister (as discussed below). It should be noted that the term *shrapnel* is commonly misused today. Shrapnel wounds are those caused by the balls and fragments of shell casing found in spherical case shot. Most references to shrapnel today actually refer to shell fragments.

Canister, or **case shot,** was the common close-range antipersonnel round fired by artillery in the Civil War (and, indeed, in most wars before the advent of modern high-explosive artillery). Canister was a simple tin can that contained a number of cast-iron balls. Lead balls, common before the Civil War, were no longer used because of the deformation of the balls and the resultant loss of effectiveness caused by the explosion of the propellant charge. The number of iron balls in the canister varied according to the gun and the range to the target (for the Napoleon there were twenty-seven balls for long-range use, ninety-two for short-range). Larger balls were used for longer-range fire (up to 600 yards was not uncommon). In many instances these larger balls were confused with grapeshot by nonartillerymen of the period (and by the uninformed to this day). The tin case broke up at the muzzle of the piece when it was fired, in effect turning the cannon into a giant shotgun. In emergencies double loads (one canister on top of the other) could be fired for a more devastating effect. This tactic was used only in true emergencies, because double-loaded canister placed severe stress on the tube, with occasionally lethal results for the gun crew.

Battery Organization

The standard Union artillery battery consisted of six guns. The Confederate artillery used a similar organization. Each gun was drawn by a limber, which carried a single ammunition chest (the chest for a Napoleon contained thirty-two rounds). In addition, each gun was accompanied by a caisson, also drawn by a limber, which together carried three additional ammunition chests. A battery forge, a battery wagon (carrying tools and equipment), and usually six reserve limber-caisson combinations (the battery ammunition reserve) completed the battery. In Confederate service the battery wagon and battery forge were usually shared between two or more batteries as an economy measure.

A gun platoon was a single piece with its limber and its accompanying limber-caisson combination. Two gun platoons made up a section; there were three sections to the battery. The members of a gun platoon included the platoon leader, who was usually a sergeant ("chief of piece"); two corporals; six enlisted men (gunners); and six drivers. A lieutenant commanded the section, and a captain commanded the battery. The battery staff included a battery adjutant, who was a lieutenant and usually commanded the line of caissons in battle; two staff sergeants (battery orderly sergeant and battery quartermaster); five artificers; two buglers; and a guidon-bearer.

Nominal full strength of a complete six-gun battery was 123. In 1861 a six-gun battery of light artillery in the Confederate service included one captain, two first lieutenants, two second lieutenants, one sergeant-major, one quartermaster-sergeant, six sergeants, twelve corporals, two buglers, one guidon-bearer, two artificers, and from 64 to 125 privates. Four-gun batteries were the same except that they had only one first lieutenant, four sergeants, and eight corporals (Wise 1959, p. 110).

A six-gun Napoleon battery would require twenty six-horse teams (six for the guns and limbers, twelve for the caissons and limbers, and two for the battery wagon and forge) and 10 spare horses. Confederate batteries often were forced to make do with four-horse teams. In a light artillery battery, the officers, sergeants, buglers, and guidon-bearer were all mounted, while the gun crews rode on the limbers or walked. Thus, 146 horses were required for a full six-gun battery. In horse artillery batteries the gunners were mounted as well.

Artillery Tactics

An artillery battery was normally deployed in a column of platoons when moving by road or across constricted terrain. When preparing to go "into battery" (that is, into a firing position), the battery was deployed into a line of gun platoons abreast. The order "action front" brought the battery into action. The guidon-bearer was placed by the battery commander to mark the right of the gun line, with the gun platoons aligned to his left. The gun platoons halted, and the guns were unlimbered and "placed into battery" (that is, the guns would be manhandled forward to the firing position). The gun-limber ammunition chests were opened, and ammunition was prepared for firing. With a good gun crew, about twenty-five seconds would elapse from the order "action front" to the time when the first round was fired.

A six-gun battery occupied a large area. According to regulations, the frontage occupied by the battery was eighty-two yards. There was a fourteen-yard interval between guns, and two yards per gun were allowed for the width of the gun carriages. The depth of the battery was forty-seven yards (five yards for the guns, with an interval of six yards; eleven yards for the gun-limber, with an interval of eleven yards; fourteen yards for the caissons) from the muzzles of the guns to the rear of the caissons. It should be remembered that these were regulation distances: tactical circumstances and the terrain usually forced modifications to this deployment. If the battery was to stay in position for some time, the horses were unharnessed and led back to a sheltered position to protect them from enemy counterbattery fire.

Whenever possible the battery deployment was staggered: one gun platoon or section might be five to ten yards forward of the next. This protected the battery from enfilade. The drill for firing a gun was a complicated but well-orchestrated ballet. Eight of the members of a gun crew were numbered, each "gun number" having a specific task in the drill. The ninth member was not numbered—he was known as the gunner and was usually the chief of piece. Numbers one and two took position at the muzzle of the piece, numbers three and four at the breech, the gunner at the trail, and numbers five, six, and seven at the limber. Number eight remained with the caissons, where he would either act as a horse-holder or as a replacement for casualties at the gun.

Numbers one and two were responsible for putting the rounds in the muzzle, ramming them home, and sponging out the barrel between rounds fired. Number three covered the vent while loading, to prevent premature detonation of the propellant charge by the hot gases forced through the vent when the round was rammed home. He also moved the trail right or left with a handspike to traverse the piece and pierced the bag of the propellant charge by inserting a prick through the vent. Number four attached the lanyard to a friction primer, inserted the primer into the vent, and pulled the lanyard to ignite the primer and so fire the gun. The gunner aimed the piece by directing the traversing done by number three. He then adjusted the elevation of the weapon and gave the order to fire. The gunner also estimated the range to the target and gave orders for the type of round and fuze-setting to be used. (In many cases, the battery commander would order the round type and fuze-setting.) Number five brought rounds from the ammunition chest to the gun, if necessary showing the gunner the round in order to confirm that the correct fuze-setting had been cut. Numbers six and seven prepared rounds, selecting the correct type that was ordered and cutting fuzes for the indicated range. All personnel assisted in the arduous task of running the guns back into position after recoil.

All the gunners were trained to act in any of the different positions if necessary. Gun drills were practiced with as few as two men to a gun. In theory, the battery drivers and staff personnel could also act as gunners to replace casualties. In practice, replacements were drawn from all possible sources, including nearby infantry and cavalry units and, in some cases, generals and their staffs.

When the ammunition in the gun-limber chest was exhausted, a full chest was brought up from the caissons. When the last chest on the caissons was brought forward and its ammunition expended, the battery would usually move as a body to the rear area designated for drawing ammunition from the army trains. It was not normal practice to send the caissons back alone for replenishment. In the heat and confusion of battle the guns could be forced to displace, a disastrous occurrence if the caissons could not locate the new gun position.

While reloading ammunition, the battery would also redistribute soldiers and horses within the gun platoons, equalizing losses caused by casualties. If losses had been severe, the battery might reduce temporarily to a smaller number of platoons, in order to maintain those platoons at full strength.

3

A Report on the Employment of the Artillery at the Battle of Antietam, Maryland, with a View to Marking Battery Positions at the Antietam National Battlefield Site
Joseph Mills Hanson

[Ed. note: This table of contents appears to have been prepared by someone other than Hanson.]

Organization of Report

I t is the primary purpose of the following report to make recommendations concerning the marking of the positions of a limited number of Federal and Confederate batteries on the battlefield of Antietam, or Sharpsburg, Maryland, with guns of Civil War type which have become available for purposes of historical display. But in order that such a report may have more permanent value than would result from the discussion of battery a few positions only, in view of the fact that at a future time guns may become available for marking other, perhaps all, important positions of the kind on this field, it has been thought advisable to somewhat extend the scope of the report. This has therefore been expanded to include a summary of the artillery equipment of both armies at Antietam and an analysis of the artillery operations sufficiently explicit to indicate in a general way the relative importance in the maneuvers of the day of at least all of the batteries on each side which figured prominently in the struggle. Such a summary of armament and analysis of operations may then be made the basis for a schedule of priority whereby the relative importance of all battery positions on the field may be determined, at least tentatively, and a logical program inaugurated looking to the eventual marking of all battery positions in the order of their importance as guns of contemporaneous date, or reproductions of such guns practicable for display purposes, shall become available for the purpose.

In order to carry out the purposes of this report as above outlined it will be necessary to divide its subject matter into several parts. These parts will be:

I.   (A). A list of the batteries of the Federal Army of the Potomac at Antietam, showing, so far as the information is obtainable, the designation of each battery, the name of its commander, the numbers and types of guns which it contained, and the higher unit to which it was attached.

(B). A list giving information similar to that indicated above in regard to the batteries of the Confederate Army of Northern Virginia at Antietam.

II.   (A). A discussion, as brief as may be consistent with clear presentation, of the activities of the individual batteries of the Confederate army, which, being on the defensive, chose their own positions and thus dictated, to a great extent, the positions which could be chosen by their opponents.

(B). A similar discussion of the employment of the individual batteries of the Federal army.

In the above discussions an effort will be made to indicate briefly the tactical effects upon the battle produced by the several batteries in their various positions.

III.   A list of battery positions in a tentative order of priority based upon the discussions in Section II. This list will be prepared as the basis for a suggested sequence of battery positions to be marked as guns for the purpose become available.

IV.   A list of suitable guns at present known to be available for marking battery positions at Antietam. [Ed. note: Not done or not available to us.]

V.   A suggested distribution to the battery positions in the order established in (III) of the guns at present available, at the rate of one gun to each position, utilizing at each, so far as possible, a gun of a type which was used at that position during the battle. [Ed. note: Not done or not available to us.]

I.

(A). Batteries of the Army of the Potomac, Major General George B. McClellan, Commanding, at the Battle of Antietam, Maryland, September 17, 1862

In an official table of organization of the Army of the Potomac on September 14–17, 1862,[1] appear the designations of the batteries belonging to that army, together with the names of the battery commanders and the brigades, divisions, and corps to which the batteries were attached. But neither in this table nor elsewhere in the *Official Records* is information given, save incidentally in a few cases, as to the numbers and types of guns which composed the various batteries.

As other available reference works consulted likewise failed to supply the desired facts, which were deemed essential for the purposes of this report, recourse was had to the Historical Section of the Army War College, Fort Humphreys, Washington, D.C. Through the cooperation of Lt. Col. Sidney S. Eberle, secretary, and Mr. Robert S. Thomas, chief clerk, of the Historical Section, the writer was placed in possession of the greater part of the information embodied in the following list of batteries of the Army of the Potomac on September 14–17, 1862, as well as with much of that contained in the notes accompanying this table and the one following it, under Section I. (B), bearing upon the artillery of the Army of Northern Virginia at the same period.

In a note by the Historical Section, Army War College, accompanying the above-mentioned material, it is stated that the latter was compiled "from various official and semi-official sources, including the Official Rebellion Records; War Department records and Returns of units; Antietam Battlefield Commission maps; Ordnance Manuals; publications by Tidball, Birkhimer, Palfrey, etc." It is therefore believed that the information assembled in [Table 1] concerning the Federal artillery at Antietam has not hitherto existed in collected form. To this information the writer has added the corps and divisions to which each battery belonged.

In explanation of some of the facts established in [Table 1], it should be pointed out that, although the official statement of the organization of the Army of the Potomac[2] gives the number of batteries in that army at Antietam as sixty-seven, as a matter of fact ten of those batteries were combined in groups of two to form single batteries under one commander. Thus the number of complete batteries enumerated in this tabulation was actually reduced to sixty-two.

But this tabulation, furthermore, failed to include the "Battery Company," or "9th Company" (Company K, 9th New York Volunteer Infantry), of five guns, under Capt. James R. Whiting; or Battery L, 2nd New York Light Artillery, six guns, under Capt. Jacob Roemer. Both of these organizations were present and in action and both are shown on the maps published by the Antietam Battlefield Board in 1904. Whiting's battery is mentioned in the official reports of General Burnside and Col. H. S. Fairchild.[3]

Although failing to account for the two batteries last mentioned, Lt. William E. Birkhimer, U.S. Army, in his work *Historical Sketch of the Organization, Administration, Matériel, and Tactics of the Artillery, United States Army,* makes the following interesting observations upon the organization of the Federal artillery at Antietam:[4]

> There accompanied the army at Antietam sixty-two batteries; seven were in reserve; fifty-five were distributed to divisions and to the XII Corps, the latter having its seven batteries organized as corps artillery, and not distributed to divisions. There were attached to the cavalry division four batteries of horse artillery (Tidball, Hains, Robertson and Gibson). Except in three divisions, one regular was associated with the volunteer batteries, in accordance with the original plan. Of the sixty-two batteries, twenty-two were regular, five of the latter being formed by uniting two distinct batteries, thus making twenty-seven the number of regular organizations represented at Antietam.

(B). Batteries of the Army of Northern Virginia, Gen. Robert E. Lee, Commanding, at the Battle of Antietam, Maryland, September 17, 1862

It is believed that no tabulation has ever been made of the batteries of the Army of Northern Virginia at Antietam, or Sharpsburg, with the num-

Table 1. Artillery: Army of the Potomac at the Battle of Antietam, or Sharpsburg, Maryland, September 17, 1862

Battery	Regiment	Commander	Number	Type	Corps	Division
				Guns		
E & G#	1st U.S.	Lt. A. N. Randol	4	12-lb. SB brass Napoleons	V	2nd
K	1st U.S.	Capt. W. M. Graham	6	12-lb. SB brass Napoleons	V	Reserve
I	1st U.S.	Lt. G. A. Woodruff	6	12-lb. SB brass Napoleons	II	2nd
A	2nd U.S.	Capt. J. C. Tidball	6	12-lb. SB brass Napoleons		Cavalry Division
B & L#	2nd U.S.	Capt. J. M. Robertson	4	12-lb. SB brass Napoleons		Cavalry Division
D	2nd U.S.	Lt. E. B. Williston	6	12-lb. SB brass Napoleons	VI	1st
E	2nd U.S.	Lt. S. N. Benjamin	4	20-lb. Parrotts (rifled)	IX	1st
G##	2nd U.S.	Lt. J. H. Butler	4	12-lb. SB brass Napoleons	IV	1st
M	2nd U.S.	Lt. P. C. Hains	6	3-in. rifles (Ordnance guns)		Cavalry Division
C & G#	3rd U.S.	Capt. H. G. Gibson	6	3-in. rifles (Ordnance guns)		Cavalry Division
L & M# ##	3rd U.S.	Capt. Jno. Edwards, Jr.	6	4 10-lb. Parrotts (rifled); 2 12-lb. howitzers	IX	Kanawha Division
A & C#	4th U.S.	Lt. Evan Thomas	6	12-lb. SB brass Napoleons	II	1st
B	4th U.S.	Capt. J. B. Campbell	6	12-lb. SB brass Napoleons	II	1st
E	4th U.S.	Lt. Joseph Stewart	6	12-lb. SB brass Napoleons	II	2nd
F	4th U.S.	Capt. J. C. Clark, Jr.	4	10-lb. Parrotts (rifled)	IX	2nd
G	4th U.S.	Lt. E. D. Muhlenberg	6	3-in. rifles (Ordnance guns)	XII	Reserve
A	5th U.S.	Lt. M. P. Miller	6	12-lb. SB brass Napoleons	V	3rd
		Lt. C. P. Muhlenberg	6	12-lb. SB brass Napoleons	IX	

continued on next page

Table 1. Continued

Battery	Regiment	Commander	Number	Type	Corps	Division
C	5th U.S.	Capt. D. R. Ranson	4	12-lb. SB brass Napoleons	I	3rd
D	5th U.S.	Lt. C. E. Hazlett	6	10-lb. Parrotts (rifled)	V	1st
F	5th U.S.	Lt. L. Martin	6	(4 10-lb. Parrotts (rifled); 2 12-lb. Howitzers	VI	2nd
I	5th U.S.	Capt. S. H. Weed	4	3-in. rifles (Ordnance guns)	V	2nd
K	5th U.S.	Lt. Wm. E. Van Reed	4	12-lb. SB brass Napoleons	V	2nd
Ky.	Simmonds's Ind.	Capt. S. Simmonds	6	4 10-lb. Parrotts (rifled); 2 20-lb. Parrotts (rifled)	IX	Kanawha Division
4th Maine	Ind.	Capt. O. W. Robinson	4	20-lb. Parrotts (rifled)	XII	Corps
6th Maine	Ind.	Capt. F. McGilvery	4	20-lb. Parrotts (rifled)	XII	Corps
A	1st Md.	Capt. J. W. Wolcott	6	3-in. rifles (Ordnance guns)	VI	1st
B	1st Md.	Lt. T. J. Vanneman	6	3-in. Rifles (Ordnance guns)	VI	2nd
First N.H.	Ind.	Lt. F. M. Edgell	6	12-lb. Howitzers	I	1st
A	1st N.J.	Capt. Wm. Hexamer	6	3-in. rifles (Ordnance guns)	VI	1st
B	1st N.Y.	Capt. R. D. Pettit	6	10-lb. Parrotts (rifled)	II	1st
C##	1st N.Y.	Capt. A. Barnes	4	3-in. rifles (Ordnance guns)	V	3rd
G	1st N.Y.	Capt. J. D. Frank	4	12-lb. brass Napoleons	II	Unatt.
L	1st N.Y.	Capt. J. A. Reynolds	6	3-in. rifles (Ordnance guns)	I	1st
M	1st N.Y.	Capt. G. W. Cothran	6	3-in. rifles (Ordnance guns)	XII	Corps

Table 1. Continued

Battery	Regiment	Commander	Number	Type	Corps	Division
				Guns		
21st N.Y.	Ind.	Capt. Andrew Cowan	4	3-in. rifles (Ordnance guns)	VI	2nd
3rd## N.Y.	Ind.	Capt. Wm. Stuart	4	10-lb. Parrotts (rifled)	IV	81st
5th N.Y.	Ind.	Capt. E. D. Taft	4	20-lb. Parrotts (rifled)	V	Reserve
10th N.Y.	Ind.	Capt. J. T. Bruen	4	12-lb. S.B. brass Napoleons	XII	Corps
L	2nd N.Y.	Capt. Jacob Roemer	6	3-in. rifles (Ordnance guns)	IX	1st
A	1st N.Y. Bn.	Lt. Bernhard Wever	4	20-lb. Parrotts (rifled)	V	Reserve
B	1st N.Y. Bn.	Lt. A. VonKleiser	4	20-lb. Parrotts (rifled)	V	Reserve
C	1st N.Y.	Capt. Robt. Langner	4	20-lb. Parrotts (rifled)	V	Reserve
D	1st N.Y.	Capt. Chas. Kusserow	4	3-in. rifles (Ordnance guns)	V	Reserve
Co. K	9th N.Y. Inf.	Capt. Jas. B. Whiting *Note:* This battery is spoken of as the "Battery Company," "Ninth Battery," etc.	5	12-lb. Dahlgren rifles (boat howitzers—brass)	IX	3rd
1st Ohio	Ind.	Capt. J. R. McMullin	6	10-lb. Parrotts (rifled)	IX	Kanawha Division
L	1st Ohio	Capt. L. N. Robinson	6	12-lb. SB brass Napoleons	V	3rd
A	1st Pa.	Lt. J. G. Simpson	4	12-lb. SB brass Napoleons	I	3rd
B	1st Pa.	Capt. J. H. Cooper	4	3-in. rifles (Ordnance guns)	I	3rd
C##	1st Pa.	Capt. J. McCarthy	4	10-lb. Parrotts (rifled)	IV	1st

continued on next page

Table 1. Continued

Battery	Regiment	Commander	Number	Type	Corps	Division
				Guns		
D##	1st Pa.	Capt. Michael Hall	4	10-lb. Parrotts (rifled)	IV	1st
F	1st Pa.	Capt. E. W. Matthews	4	3-in. rifles (Ordnance guns)	I	2nd
G##	1st Pa.	Capt. Frank P. Amsden	4	3-in. rifles (Ordnance guns)	I	3rd
C	Pa. Light	Capt. Jas. Thompson	4	3-in. rifles (Ordnance guns)	I	2nd
D	Pa. Light	Capt. G. W. Durell	6	10-lb. Parrotts (rifled)	IX	2nd
E	Pa. Light	Capt. Jos. M. Knap	6	3-in. rifles (Ordnance guns)	XII	Corps
F	Pa. Light	Capt. Robt. B. Hampton	4	3-in. rifles (Ordnance guns)	XII	Corps
A	1st R.I.	Capt. J. A. Tompkins	6	10-lb. Parrotts (rifled)	II	2nd
B	1st. R.I.	Capt. J. G. Hazard	6	12-lb. SB brass Napoleons	II	Unatt.
C	1st R.I.	Capt. R. Waterman	4	12-lb. SB brass Napoleons	V	1st
D	1st R.I.	Capt. J. A. Monroe	6	12-lb. SB brass Napoleons	I	1st
G	1st R.I.	Capt. C. D. Owen	6	3-in. rifles (Ordnance guns)	II	Unatt.

Total U.S. regular army batteries   22 batteries, 116 guns
Total U.S. volunteer batteries   42 batteries, 207 guns

# Indicates two units combined to form one battery.
Indicates not present or not engaged in the battle.

Recapitulation

Batteries

Total number of batteries	69	323 guns
Ten U.S. regular army batteries combined to form five batteries	5	26 guns
Total number of complete batteries	64	323 guns
Batteries not present or not engaged	7	30 guns
Batteries present and engaged	57	293 guns

Guns

Type	Present	Absent	Total
20-lb. Parrott guns (rifled)	30	0	30
10-lb. Parrott guns (rifled)	42	16	58
12-lb. howitzers (U.S. model)	14	2	16
12-lb. SB brass (bronze) Napoleons	108	4	112
3-in. rifles (Ordnance guns)	94	8	102
12-lb. Dahlgren boat howitzers (rifled)	5	0	5
Total	**293**	**30**	**323**

Total U.S. regular army batteries	22 batteries, 116 guns
Total U.S. volunteer batteries	42 batteries, 207 guns

bers and types of guns which they contained, which is more than approximately correct. With the data which exist probably no absolutely accurate list can ever be made. The tabulation by Gen. William N. Pendleton, chief of artillery, Army of Northern Virginia,[5] seems to have been prepared after November 7, 1862, and it contains many discrepancies which become apparent when it is compared with the table entitled "Organization of the Army of Northern Virginia during the Maryland Campaign."[6] The table last mentioned shows batteries not listed by Pendleton, and vice versa, while statements of the grouping of batteries in higher units differ greatly in the two documents.

Utilizing both Pendleton's list and the table of organization last referred to, Colonel Jennings C. Wise, in his work *The Long Arm of Lee*,[7] draws some valuable conclusions concerning the organization and armament of the Confederate artillery during the Maryland campaign. But he does not attempt to separate the batteries which were at Antietam from those which were not, while certain errors have crept into his quoted tables which render them not altogether reliable.

General Pendleton either tabulates or names as unaccounted for eighty-four batteries in the Army of Northern Virginia as of "the summer of 1862, at Sharpsburg, Etc." This figure includes many batteries which did not participate in the battle. In a footnote (p. 837) to Pendleton's tables it is shown that these tables account for a total of 271 guns of all types. But these are the guns only of the sixty-one batteries which are tabulated, while the guns of twenty-three other batteries are not given.

The Historical Section, Army War College, has advised the writer, though without quoting the source of its information, that "the best compilation of the batteries and guns of the Army of Northern Virginia at the time of the battle of Antietam, shows that there were 77 batteries with 293 guns of all types, many of which were not present during the engagement of September 17, 1862."

In [Table 2] the writer has endeavored to show, on the basis of information gathered from all available sources, the Confederate batteries only which were actually on the field at Antietam, whether or not the numbers and types of their guns are known. Arrived at in this way the list shows in Longstreet's Corps twenty-one batteries known to have contained 95 guns together with five batteries the armament of which are unknown. In Jackson's Corps it shows seventeen batteries with 66 guns known and two batteries the numbers and types of whose guns are unknown. In the reserve artillery it shows six batteries with 33 guns and three batteries, guns unknown. In the Cavalry Division it shows three batteries, guns unknown.

The [figures in Table 2] give a total for the Confederate army on the field at Antietam of forty-four batteries with a known armament of 194 guns and thirteen batteries whose armament is unknown. It is reasonable to assume an average of 4 guns each in the batteries of unknown armament since the average in the other forty-four batteries was 4.4 guns per battery. This would give 52 guns in the thirteen batteries, or a grand total of fifty-seven batteries with 246 guns present on the field at Antietam.

It is interesting to note that each of the two armies had fifty-seven batteries actively engaged. But in their batteries the Federals had a preponderance of 47 guns, while their pieces, on the average, considerably exceeded those of the Confederates in range and weight of metal thrown.

It will be noticed that the [estimates in Table 2] show a considerably smaller number of Confederate batteries and guns at Antietam than does that of the Historical Section, Army War College. But the Historical Section estimate admittedly includes many batteries which were not present at the battle. The present estimate also eliminates the considerable number of batteries carried in General Pendleton's tabulation which are known to have been absent from the battle, while it adds certain others, omitted by him, which are known to have been present. While absolute accuracy is not claimed for the new estimate, it is believed that it accounts more closely than previous ones for the Confederate artillery actually on the field at Antietam.

It will be remembered that in the [Recapitulation] list the only batteries named are those which are believed to have participated in the battle. Of the thirty-one batteries properly belonging to Longstreet's Corps, five had been detached earlier in the campaign and were absent, while twenty-six were present, as indicated above. In Jackson's Corps, of a total of twenty-four batteries, five were absent and nineteen present. The general artillery reserve of the army consisted of three battalions of five batteries each, one battalion of four batteries, and a miscellaneous group of four batteries. Two of the five-battery battalions and three of the miscellaneous batteries were absent, a total of thirteen batteries absent. The remaining five-battery battalion, less one battery, was present, as were the four-battery battalion and one of the miscellaneous batteries. Hence, of a total of twenty-three reserve batteries, fourteen were absent and nine present. The three horse batteries of the cavalry were all present.

II.

(A). Discussion of the Employment of the Confederate Artillery at Antietam

Upon retiring from the passes of South Mountain on the night of September 14, 1862, General Lee marched the portion of his army under General Longstreet toward the Potomac River near Sharpsburg, Maryland. With the purpose of offering battle to the Army of the Potomac under General McClellan, Lee began concentrating his forces on the plateau west of Antietam Creek, with the Potomac in his rear.

He posted Longstreet's troops on the right of his line extending, inclusive of the flank guard consisting of Munford's brigade of Stuart's cavalry, from the confluence of the Antietam and the Potomac to a point about a mile northeast of Sharpsburg. When Jackson, who had captured Harpers Ferry on September 15, arrived at Sharpsburg with a part of his troops on the morning of the sixteenth, Lee placed him on the left of the line of battle, extending from Longstreet's left to a point roughly a mile and a half north of Sharpsburg and less than a mile from the Potomac. The interval between Jackson's left flank and the river was filled by two of the three brigades of Stuart's cavalry.

On September 16 the artillery of each corps was placed in firing or support positions along the front of its own corps. However, until the arrival at different times during September 17 of the balance of the troops

Table 2. Artillery: Army of Northern Virginia at the Battle of Antietam, or Sharpsburg, Maryland, September 17, 1862

	20-lb. Parrotts	10-lb. Parrotts	3-in. rifles	24-lb. howitzers	12-lb. howitzers	12-lb. Napoleons	Whitworths	Blakelys	6-lb. S.B. guns	Total
Longstreet's Corps (Right Wing) *—Col. H. C. Cabell, chief of artillery*										
McLaws's Division										
Maj. S. P. Hamilton, chief of artillery										
Manly's (N.C.) Bty., Capt. B. C. Manly			1		2				3	6
Pulaski (Ga.) Bty., Capt. J. P. W. Read		1	1						1	3
Richmond Fayette (Va.) Bty., Capt. M. C. Macon		2							4	6
Richmond Howitzers, 1st Co. (Va.) Capt. E. S. McCarthy		2							2	4
Troop (Ga.) Bty., Capt. H. H. Carlton		2			1				2	5
Anderson's Division										
Maj. J. S. Saunders, chief of artillery										
Donaldsonville (La.) Bty., Capt. V. Maurin		2	1						3	6
Huger's Norfolk (Va.) Bty., Capt. C. R. Phelps		1	1						2	4
Lynchburg (Va.) Bty., Capt. M. N. Moorman										—
Grimes's Portsmouth (Va.) Bty., Lt. J. H. Thompson										—
D. R. Jones Division										
Wise (Va.) Bty., Capt. J. S. Brown										—
Walker's Division										
Petersburg (Va.) Bty., Capt. J. R. Branch		1	2		3					6
Stafford (Va.) Bty., Capt. D. A. French		3			3					6

Table 2. Continued

Hood's Division

Maj B. W. Frobel, chief of artillery

Battery	20-lb. Parrotts	10-lb. Parrotts	3-in. rifles	24-lb. howitzers	12-lb. howitzers	12-lb. Napoleons	Whitworths	Blakelys	6-lb. S.B. guns	Total
Charleston (S.C.) "German" Bty., Capt. W. K. Bachman						4				4
Palmetto (S.C.) Bty., Capt. H. R. Garden					1	1			2	4
Rowan (N.C.) Bty., Capt. J. Reilly		2	2	2						6
Macbeth (S.C.) Bty., Capt. R. Boyce										—
First Reserve Battalion (Corps Artillery)										
Col. J. B. Walton, commanding										
1st Co., Washington Arty. (La.) Capt. C. W. Squires		2	2							4[a]
2nd Co., Washington Arty. (La.) Capt. J. B. Richardson					2	2				4
3rd Co., Washington Arty. (La.) Capt. M. B. Miller						4				4[b]
4th Co., Washington Arty. (La.) Capt. B. F. Eshleman					2				2	4
Second Reserve Battalion (Corps Artillery)										
Col S. D. Lee, commanding										
Ashland, (Va.) Bty., Capt. P. Woolfolk, Jr.										—
Bedford (Va.) Bty., Capt. T. C. Jordan			2		1				1	4
Brooks (Rhett's) (S.C.) Bty., Lt. W. Elliott	2	2								4
Bath (Va.) Bty., Capt. J. L. Eubank			1		1				1	3
Madison (La.) Bty., Capt. G. V. Moody			2	2						4
Richmond (Va.) Bty., Capt. W. W. Parker			2		2					4

continued on next page

Table 2. Continued

Jackson's Corps (Left Wing)
—Col. S. Crutchfield, chief of artillery

Battery	20-lb. Parrotts	10-lb. Parrotts	3-in. rifles	24-lb. howitzers	12-lb. howitzers	12-lb. Napoleons	Whitworths	Blakelys	6-lb. S.B. guns	Total
Ewell's Division *Maj. A. R. Courtney, chief of artillery*										
Charlottesville (Va.) Bty., Capt. J. D. Carrington			2		2				4	
Staunton (Va.) (Balthis's) Bty., Capt. A. W. Garber									2	2
1st Maryland (Md.) Bty., Capt. W. F. Dement						4				4
Bedford (Va.) Bty., Capt. J. R. Johnson		1	2							
Louisiana Guard (La.) Bty., Capt. L. E. D'Aquin		1				2				3
A. P. Hill's Light Division *Lt. Col. R. L. Walker, chief of artillery*										
Richmond (Va.) Bty., Capt. W. D. Crenshaw					1	1			2	4
Fredericksburg (Va.) Bty., Capt. C. M. Braxton			2		1				4	6
Pee Dee (S.C.) Bty., Capt. D. G. McIntosh		1	1			1				4
Richmond "Purcell" (Va.) Bty., Capt. W. J. Pegram		2				2				4
Jackson's (J. R. Jones's) Division *Maj. L. M. Shumaker, chief of artillery*										
Baltimore (Second Md.) Bty., Capt. J. B. Brockenbrough			1			1		2		4
Lynchburg "Lee" (Va.) Bty., Capt. C. J. Raine			3		1					4
First Rockbridge (Va.) Bty., Capt. W. T. Poague		2				1				3[c]

Table 2. Continued

	20-lb. Parrotts	10-lb. Parrotts	3-in. rifles	24-lb. howitzers	12-lb. howitzers	12-lb. Napoleons	Whitworths	Blakelys	6-lb. S.B. guns	Total
Jackson's (J. R. Jones's) Division (*cont.*)										
Alleghany (Va.) Bty., Capt. J. Carpenter			2			2				4
Danville (Va.) Bty., Capt. G. W. Wooding		2	1			1				4
Hampden (Va.) Bty., Capt. W. H. Caskie		1							3	4
D. H. Hill's Division										
Maj. S. F. Pierson, chief of artillery										
Alabama (Ala.) Bty., Capt. R. A. Hardaway			2				1			3
Jeff. Davis (Ala.) Bty., Capt. J. W. Bondurant			2		2					4
Peninsula (Va.) Bty., Capt. W. B. Jones										—
King William (Va.) Bty., Capt. T. H. Carter		1			2				2	5
General Reserve Artillery of the Army										
—*Brig. Gen. W. N. Pendleton, chief of artillery*										
Cutts's Battalion										
Lt. Col. A. S. Cutts, commanding										
Bty. D, Sumter Bn. (Ga.), Capt. J. A. Blackshear					3				3	6
Bty. E, Sumter Bn. (Ga.), Capt. J. Lane	2	3					1			6
Bty. B, Sumter Bn. (Ga.), Capt. G. M. Patterson										—
Bty. A, Sumter Bn. (Ga.), Capt. H. M. Ross		3			2	1				6

Continued on next page

Table 2. Continued

	20-lb. Parrotts	10-lb. Parrotts	3-in. rifles	24-lb. howitzers	12-lb. howitzers	12-lb. Napoleons	Whitworths	Blakelys	6-lb. S.B. guns	Total
Jones's Battalion										
Maj. H. P. Jones, commanding										
Louis "Morris" (Va.) Bty., Capt. R. C. M. Page			2		1				3	6
Richmond "Orange" (Va.) Bty., Capt. J. Peyton			1		1				3	5
Goochland (Va.) Bty., Capt. W. H. Turner										—
"Long Island" (Va.) Bty., Capt. A. Wimbish										—
Miscellaneous Batteries										
Winchester (Va.) Bty., Capt. W. E. Cutshaw			2		2					4
Stuart Horse Artillery										
Capt. John Pelham, commanding										
"Ashby" (Va.) Bty., Capt. R. P. Chew										—
"Washington" (S.C.) Bty., Capt. J. F. Hart										—
"First Stuart" (Va.) Bty., Capt. J. Pelham										—

[a] Walton's report, *O.R.*, vol. 19, pt. 1, p. 848. Pendleton (ibid., p. 836) gives Squires 1 10-lb. Parrott and 2 3-in. rifles; total, 3 guns.

[b] Walton's report, ibid., p. 848. Pendleton (ibid., p. 836) gives Miller 2 12-lb. Napoleons; total, 2 guns.

[c] Poague's report, ibid., p. 837) gives Poague 2 20-lb Parrotts and 2 10-lb Parrotts; total, 4 guns.

Recapitulation

Guns

Type	Present
20-lb. Parrott guns (rifled)	4
10-lb. Parrott guns (rifled)	36
3-in. guns (rifled)	40
24-lb. howitzers (smoothbore)	4
12-lb. howitzers (smoothbore)	34
12-lb. Napoleons (smoothbore)	27
2.71-in. Whitworths (rifled)	2
3.5-inch Blakelys (smoothbore)	2
[Ed. note: This is an obvious error. The line should read "Blakelys (rifled)."]	
6-lb. guns (smoothbore)	45
Total guns, known calibers	194
Guns of unknown calibers in 13 batteries, assuming 4 guns per battery	52
Grand total	**246**

which had been with Jackson at Harpers Ferry, not all of the artillery which later participated in the battle came upon the field, and A. P. Hill's Light Division, of Jackson's Corps, with four batteries, eighteen guns, did not reach there until its decisive appearance south of Sharpsburg on the afternoon of the seventeenth.

On the afternoon of September 16 General McClellan ordered General Hooker with the I Corps to cross the Antietam a mile and a half northeast of Sharpsburg and to attack the Confederate left. There resulted a spirited artillery duel lasting until dark, though Hooker did not press his attack and no material changes of position occurred. But immediately after daylight on the morning of the seventeenth, Hooker pushed forward the lines of battle of his three divisions, about 12,000 men, and fiercely attacked Jackson, who had about 5,500 men in position.

Hooker's advance was directly supported by the ten batteries belonging to the I Corps and indirectly by the fire of the mass of guns, about seventy-five in number, many of them 20-lb. Parrott rifles, of General Hunt's artillery reserve, posted along the hills east of the Antietam, some 3,000 yards from Jackson's position, which faced generally northeast in the vicinity of the Dunkard Church. Hunt's batteries thus had an enfilade fire on Jackson's lines, an advantage which they utilized to the full by a constant heavy fire.[8]

At this time the Confederate batteries of Poague, Carpenter, Brockenbrough, Raine, Caskie, and Wooding,[9] with those of Parker, Woolfolk, and Rhett, of S. D. Lee's battalion, firing at close range from near the Dunkard Church, made it possible for the infantry of J. R. Jones's and Lawton's divisions to stop Hooker's first attack and drive the assailants back upon their supporting artillery.[10] A section of Jordan's battery under Capt. J. S. Taylor, pressing boldly forward in pursuit, was, however, thrown back by overwhelming fire.[11]

The nine batteries just mentioned, joined by Pelham's, of the horse artillery,[12] were now, about 6:45 A.M., called upon to face a second determined attack by Hooker. Jones's division, now under Grigsby, and Lawton's were pushed back as far as in the first attack but Hood's division came to their aid on the right of Lawton, accompanied by three batteries of Frobel's battalion, Bachman's, Garden's, and Reilly's.[13] Bachman galloped out into the cornfield north of the Dunkard Church, scene of much of the most desperate fighting on this part of the field, and opened on the Federals at 150 yards.[14] But in a few minutes Hooker's skirmishers, creeping within 50 yards, forced Bachman to retire with the loss of many men and horses.[15]

The Federals still continuing to press their advance, D. H. Hill, on Jackson's right, sent three brigades to Hood's assistance.[16] In consequence Hooker's troops, for the second time, were thrown back upon their artillery line. Having supported this Confederate recovery of ground the batteries of Woolfolk, Parker, and Rhett, badly damaged and with ammunition exhausted, were ordered to the rear to refit.[17] Moody's battery was the only one available to replace them. One section of this battery galloped forward into a ploughed field in advance of the infantry and for fifteen minutes fired destructively upon the enemy.[18]

Between 8:30 and 9:00 A.M. Mansfield's XII Corps, approaching rapidly, reinforced Hooker's exhausted troops.[19] On the Confederate side Early's brigade joined the remnants of Jones's division in the West Woods, while J. G. Walker's two brigades and the brigade of G. T. Anderson, from Longstreet's right, came into line between Hood and Jones.[20] The Confederate position was greatly exposed but in the interval between Hooker's and Mansfield's attacks, Pelham, to whom Jackson had sent several additional batteries,[21] moved his own, Poague's, Raine's, and Brockenbrough's batteries, joined later by D'Aquin's, into a position in rear and to the left of Jones's line, where he could sweep all the ground between the Nicodemus house and the Dunkard Church.[22]

Pelham's maneuver was one of the most skillful and effective of the battle, for the ground he chose for his guns was completely protected from the fire of Hunt's batteries beyond the Antietam, while his own guns swept the entire terrain over which Mansfield's attack would have to pass and thus perfectly secured the left of the Confederate infantry line.[23] The advance of Mansfield through Hooker's shattered lines again forced Hood and the units on his flanks out of the thirty-acre cornfield, across the Hagerstown pike, and to the Dunkard Church. Greene's division, forming Mansfield's left, reached the church but the right could not progress across the zone swept by Pelham's guns, and was driven back to the East Woods.[24]

General Lee at this juncture sent his last reserves on the field, McLaws's and R. H. Anderson's divisions of Longstreet, into the fight, the former to the aid of Jackson near the Dunkard Church, the latter to the support of D. H. Hill on the right of Jackson.[25] Moody's and Jordan's batteries, badly cut up, had gone to the rear to refit,[26] leaving Hill protecting the Confederate center along the ridge between the church and Sharpsburg with, so far as artillery was concerned, his four divisional batteries under Hardaway, Bondurant, Jones, and Carter, and the four reserve batteries of Cutts's battalion under Lane, Blackshear, Patterson, and Ross.[27]

Following promptly across the Antietam behind Mansfield, the Federal II Corps, under Sumner, now, at 9:30 A.M. or a little after,[28] came upon the field. Sumner's division under Sedgwick attacked westward over the same ground on which Hooker and Mansfield had been repulsed, but the divisions of French and Richardson deflected to the left and drove Hill's advanced units southward from the vicinity of the Roulette and Clipp buildings to the sunken road since called the "Bloody Lane."[29] Early, Jones and McLaws met Sedgwick's impetuous charge into the West Woods and, getting upon his flanks, after a ferocious struggle drove him, like his predecessors, back to the vicinity of the East Woods.[30]

As Sumner's divisions had arrived their artillery had been constantly augmented by additional batteries which furnished superb support to the infantry, but could not break down Pelham's group or prevent other Confederate batteries, though badly outmatched, from giving the same sort of aid to the gray infantry. Thus when McLaws followed up Sedgwick in a counterattack he was closely accompanied by his five divisional batteries under Manly, Read, Macon, McCarthy, and Carlton. Of these, Read's went into such close action in the open on the right on the West Woods that it lost fourteen officers and men and sixteen horses in a quarter of an hour.[31] Carlton's battery was nearly cut to pieces by the Federal artillery fire.[32]

The arrival of Smith's division of Franklin's VI Corps checked the Confederates following up Sedgwick's repulsed troops and well before noon the terrible infantry battle in this quarter virtually ended, though the artillery duel continued unabated for hours. Jackson and those who had come to his aid retained possession of the West Woods under the protecting fire of Pelham's artillery group and the divisional batteries on that part of the field, while the Federal line held the East Woods beyond the cornfield with some fifteen batteries along their front and on their right flank.[33] In probably less than six hours of battle Jackson, with about 19,500 men and 40 guns, had virtually held his position at a loss of 5,754 men, 29 percent of his troops engaged. The Federals had engaged about 30,500 infantry and 100 guns, besides those of Hunt across the Antietam, and had lost about 7,000 officers and men in casualties.[34]

Meanwhile, with the advance of French and Richardson against D. H. Hill in front of the Bloody Lane, the vortex of the battle shifted toward the center. From the fields and ravines north of the lane Hill was forced back into the latter. Finally, after a savage struggle there, he was driven southwest to the fields and orchard of the Piper farm. In his desperate defense of the lane Hill was gallantly supported by a number of batteries, among them those of Hardaway, Bondurant, W. B. Jones, and Carter, of his own divisional artillery battalion and others of Cutts's and Jones's reserve battalions.[35] Regardless of the fire of Hunt's guns these batteries clung to exposed positions on the ridge west of the Hagerstown pike until fairly swept from them by the Federal fire.[36] Longstreet then ordered Miller's battery of the Washington Artillery to Hill's aid. Going into action immediately in rear of Hill's line Miller was once driven off with the loss of a number of his men, but returned with two guns and for half an hour held the hostile infantry in check until again driven away.[37]

After Hill had been forced to retire to the southeast of the Piper house Miller, joined by another gun and a caisson of ammunition, went in once more near that house, supported by a handful of infantry, and poured canister into Richardson's lines.[38] At this juncture Miller's battery, with the infantry around it, was almost the only defense remaining between the advancing enemy and Sharpsburg. Federal horse batteries of Pleasonton's cavalry, approaching on its right flank along the Boonsboro pike from the Middle Bridge, took Miller under fire and as his unit came to the verge of exhaustion through losses of personnel, General Longstreet and his staff rode up. While Longstreet held their horses the members of his staff aided the cannoneers in working the guns until the ammunition was expended.[39]

Now, just in the nick of time, at about 1:00 P.M., Boyce's battery appeared on the scene, enabling Miller to finally retire. Boyce galloped within a few yards of the Federal lines and rapidly fired canister into them but itself lost nineteen men and fifteen horses.[40] Hill's infantry, however, having somewhat recovered itself and assisted by Boyce's fire and that of other batteries further to the rear, now advanced sufficiently to repossess itself of the Piper buildings and orchard, while the Federals retired to the Bloody Lane or beyond.[41] Here, reinforced by fresh batteries, they again endeavored to advance but were prevented by the four batteries of Saunders's battalion, Moorman's, Maurin's, Phelps's, and Thompson's, which replaced Lee's battalion as the latter, for the second time, retired to refit.[42]

At about 2:00 in the afternoon a determined effort was begun by troops of Pleasonton's cavalry division and Sykes's division of United States Regulars, supported by four batteries of regular artillery, to capture the ridge immediately east of Sharpsburg by an advance along the Boonsboro pike. The formidable offensive was opposed at first almost solely by vigorous fire from Squires's and Garden's batteries, posted on the crest at the eastern entrance to the town, which had hardly any infantry near to help them.[43] But by 3:30 P.M. the attack, several times resumed, had been definitely frustrated by these batteries, gradually reinforced by such pieces of Moody's, Jordan's, and Rhett's batteries of Lee's battalion as had been able to partly refit and return to the field.[44] Garnett's brigade then advanced and forced the Federals back toward the Middle Bridge.

Southeast of Sharpsburg the main Federal effort was directed by Burnside's IX Corps at getting across Antietam Creek on the bridge later called the "Burnside Bridge." This effort was successfully carried through about 1:00 P.M. by Sturgis's division, though bitterly opposed by Toombs's brigade, closely backed by the fire of Eubanks's and Richardson's batteries. Soon after Sturgis's crossing Rodman's division got over at Snavely's Ford, farther down stream, against the resistance of Eshleman's battery, and closed up on the left of Willcox's division, which had relieved that of Sturgis. Thereupon the Federals began advancing in line of battle across the hills toward Sharpsburg, supported by three batteries on the field besides those firing from east of the Antietam.

The Confederates, forced slowly back toward Sharpsburg, were reinforced by Bachman's and Reilly's batteries of Hood's division, returning to the field, and by Brown's battery of Jones's division.[45] Garden's battery, just east of Sharpsburg, now also faced south and joined by one section of Reilly checked Willcox for a time at a range of 100 yards.[46] In a few moments their ammunition was exhausted and all but three pieces were disabled. The injured guns were run to the rear by hand and barely escaped the Federal skirmishers as Reilly's second section arrived and, enfilading the Federal left with canister, threw it back momentarily.[47]

Nevertheless, hardly any Confederate infantry was on the ground and the Federal line swept onward almost into the streets of Sharpsburg. But batteries from the left and center came galloping to join those already in action to save Lee's right from destruction until A. P. Hill's Light Division which now, at about 3:30 P.M., was rapidly approaching from Harpers Ferry, could deploy and beat back the Federal offensive.

Preceding Hill's infantry his four batteries, Braxton's, Pegram's, McIntosh's, and Crenshaw's, hurried upon the field and unlimbering close to the Federal line of battle opened a destructive fire upon the assailants' flank.[48] Cutshaw's independent reserve battery and Dement's, of Ewell's division, also appear to have come upon the field.[49]

The Federal infantry drove McIntosh's men from their guns but the latter were recovered when Hill's three brigades under Archer, Branch, and Gregg deployed and charged across the fields, driving back the Federals of Rodman's division toward the bridge.[50] Braxton's battery, with one piece of Pegram's, now got a position from which it poured an enfilade fire down Willcox's line at a range of about 500 yards, while surviving elements of the batteries of Bachman, Miller, Reilly, Richardson, Squires, and Eshleman, together with Cutshaw's, assailed them from the west.[51] This resulted in the whole Federal line retiring upon more sheltered positions close to the bridge. By about 5:30 P.M. the battle south of Sharpsburg was virtually over.

It is evident that, owing either to mere coincidence whereby mention of certain active batteries was omitted from all the Confederate official reports which have survived, or perhaps to failure of certain commanding officers to report at all, some artillery organizations of Lee's army which must have borne conspicuous parts in the battle are not mentioned in any way in the official narratives of the battle. This is the case, for example, with the reserve battalion of Major H. P. Jones, consisting of Peyton's, Turner's, Wimbish's, and R. C. M. Page's batteries. It is merely stated in a footnote in the *Official Records*[52] that the battalion was with D. H. Hill's division at Sharpsburg, and though Wise[53] named the battalion as present on the field he did so without making reference to any specific action on its part.

Yet on every one of the fourteen situation maps prepared by Colonel E. B. Cope for the Antietam Battlefield Board the batteries of Jones's battalion are shown in positions just east of the Hagerstown pike, near the Piper farm buildings and within 700 yards of Bloody Lane; as indicated on these maps the changes of position of the four batteries from the beginning to the end of the battle did not extend over an area more than 300 or 400 yards square. Facing eastward, early in the conflict, toward the Middle Bridge, by 9:00 A.M., when French's and Richardson's attacks fell on D. H. Hill along Bloody Lane, the guns faced northeast and supported Hill's men in their desperate struggle at and behind the lane. By 12:15 P.M., with the advance of Sykes's division and some of

Pleasonton's batteries along the Boonsboro pike, they again faced east and fought, with the Washington Artillery and other units, against this offensive until it was driven back, Jones's guns being at times almost in the midst of the Confederate infantry. The close of the battle, according to the maps, found them just east of the Piper buildings, facing the advanced Federal lines.

(B). Discussion of the Employment
of the Federal Artillery at Antietam

When the I Army Corps under General Hooker on the afternoon of September 16, 1862, crossed the Antietam at the Upper Bridge and the ford immediately below it, near Keedysville, Maryland, it was accompanied by the artillery of its three divisions, numbering ten batteries. These were the batteries of Edgell, Monroe, Reynolds, Campbell, Matthews, Thompson, Simpson, Cooper, Ransom, and Amsden. Soon after daybreak on the morning of the seventeenth, after a heavy exchange of fire with the Confederate artillery,[54] most of the Federal batteries advanced with the infantry assaulting lines into the open ground about 1,000 yards north of the Dunkard Church, between the East Woods and the West Woods.

Accompanying the advance brigades of Doubleday's and Ricketts's divisions in their forward sweep into the cornfield, Thompson's battery[55] took post in the latter while Campbell's finally occupied an exposed position just west of the Hagerstown pike. From these positions the canister of the two batteries drove back a part of Jackson's battle line.[56] Captain Campbell being wounded, Lieutenant Stewart took his battery, but so many men and horses had been killed and wounded by Confederate sharpshooters that the battery was ordered out of action by General Gibbon at about 7:30 A.M.[57]

Edgell's battery followed the advanced ones into the plowed ground just north of the cornfield and soon thereafter Matthews, Monroe, Ransom, and Reynolds also pushed forward into the same area,[58] accompanying the 2nd Division, under Ricketts. Thompson's and Matthews's batteries were especially commended by Ricketts[59] for their destructive fire on the enemy and their endurance of heavy losses.

By 7:00 A.M. the XII Corps, commanded by General Williams after the fall of General Mansfield, had marched upon the field and engaged both of its divisions. Advancing to relieve the expended divisions of Hooker, the infantry of the XII Corps immediately became involved with Jackson's forces in a terrific struggle in which it was energetically aided by the three batteries of corps artillery under the command of Captain Best, which were present. They were the batteries of Knap, Cothran, and Hampton. The three went in to strengthen the batteries of the I Corps just north of the cornfield, facing the enemy in the West Woods, and remained in action until late in the afternoon.[60] Shortly after its arrival one section of Knap's battery, ordered in advance of the East Woods within 600 yards of the Dunkard Church, encountered the Confederate infantry in the woods and lost one of its 3-in. rifles. The battery, however, subsequently brought off the field a 12-lb. howitzer and caisson of the enemy.[61]

The II Corps under General Sumner began to arrive on the battlefield about 9:00 A.M., deploying and coming into action to the left of Hooker and Williams. Sedgwick's division, in the lead, striking almost directly westward toward the Dunkard Church and the West Woods, at first drove Early, Kershaw, and D. R. Jones back through the woods. Being vigorously supported by Greene's division, XII Corps, already on the ground, Sedgwick seized the area around the church. The II Corps batteries of Tompkins, Woodruff,[62] Owen, Frank, and Thomas, joined by batteries of the I and XII Corps such as Monroe's, Edgell's, Knap's, and Cothran's, which had been previously engaged, gallantly accompanied the infantry to the very front lines and in the vicinity of "the burning buildings" of the Mumma farm fought at ranges as short as 300 yards with the Confederate batteries of Patterson, McCarthy, and others, as well as with the more distant groups of S. D. Lee and Pelham.[63]

The contest here was prolonged and bitter in the extreme, but the Confederates succeeded in containing what at first threatened to become a clean breakthrough by Sedgwick, and before 1:00 P.M. had forced their assailants back to the edge of the East Woods. Here a strong infantry line, composed mainly of troops of the VI Corps, under Franklin, which had followed Sumner, was stretched from the vicinity of the Mumma buildings northwest to the Joseph Poffenberger farm, protecting a formidable line of batteries. The latter, which lay in position throughout the afternoon, consisted of the batteries of Martin, Hexamer, Wolcott, Vanneman, and Cowan, of the VI Corps, with those of Thomas, Frank, and Owen, of the II Corps.[64] Other batteries which had been heavily engaged earlier in the day lay a few hundred yards further back, in support.

On the extreme right of the Federal position, on high ground north of Poffenberger's, commanding the open space nearly a mile wide extending to the Potomac, lay another concentration of artillery consisting of all ten of the batteries of the I Corps, together with several of those of the XII Corps.[65]

The artillery group first mentioned, covering the East Woods, was the decisive factor which prevented either Longstreet or Jackson from attacking the Federal right center during the afternoon of the seventeenth.[66] Similarly, the group north of Poffenberger's was the factor which, despite the energy and ingenuity of Pelham and others of Lee's resourceful artillerists, forbade any attempt to turn the extreme Federal right on the seventeenth or again on the eighteenth.[67] The failure of four corps in waves of attack to break Jackson on the morning of the seventeenth was certainly not attributable to lack of self-sacrificing support on the part of the twenty or more batteries which accompanied the infantry into the "artillery hell" north of the Dunkard Church. When the infantry had finally lost its aggressive edge and resigned itself to a watchful defensive, it was this same artillery which preserved McClellan's entire right flank inviolate.

As has been said under Part II, Section (A) of this report, the attack of French's and Richardson's divisions of Sumner's corps fell upon D. H. Hill in the Bloody Lane about 9:30 A.M., and the vortex of the battle shifted rather quickly to the center of the battlefield. The offensive of these divisions, which finally cleared the lane and forced the Confederates back beyond the Piper buildings, lacked the artillery support which it should have had, else Hill might not have been able to stop his retirement even at the Hagerstown pike.[68] Graham's battery, of the V Corps, specially detailed from the reserve artillery of the army,[69] did its best to furnish close support for Richardson's division, while the attacking infantry was somewhat sustained by cross fire on the left of Hill's position from certain of Hancock's, Sumner's, and Franklin's batteries east of the Dunkard Church, at ranges of 500 yards and upward. Hill's right was also partly enfiladed by fire from the Federal reserve batteries east of the Antietam, about 2,000 yards distant.

Soon after the capture of the Bloody Lane, Pleasonton's cavalry division crossed the Antietam at the Middle Bridge. His horse batteries under Tidball, Robertson, Hains, and Gibson came into action and thrust a core of fire into the interval between D. H. Hill's right and the left of D. R. Jones's division, which was holding the hillcrests immediately east of Sharpsburg. This occurred about 1:00 P.M., just as Toombs's brigade, of Jones, was being driven from the neighborhood of the Burnside Bridge by the attack of Sturgis's division, of Burnside's IX Corps. The advance of the cavalry and its batteries, however, owing to lack of infantry support, was not pushed far enough to influence Burnside's advance.[70]

The offensive of Burnside's corps on the Federal left was, nevertheless, very heavily supported by artillery. On the steep hills forming a rough semicircle around the eastern approaches to the Burnside Bridge the IX Corps batteries of Clark, Durell, Cook, Benjamin, C. P. Muhlen-

berg, Roemer, and McMullin concentrated strong fire on the slopes west of
the bridge held by Toombs's brigade. But they were unable to derive much
advantage from their superiority in numbers and weight of metal over the
Confederate batteries of Richardson, Brown and others further back on
the hills toward Sharpsburg until after Burnside's infantry had forced the
passage of the bridge and begun clearing a bridgehead on the west side.
Clark, Durell, and Muhlenberg then went over, followed a little later by
Cook.[71] Whiting, also, crossed below with Rodman's division, at Snavely's
Ford, but seems soon to have returned to the east bank.[72] These batteries
gained the crest of the ridge some 500 yards west of the deep and narrow
creek valley and thence supported the further advance of the infantry as it
pushed forward almost into the southern edge of Sharpsburg.[73]

In view of the great shortage of Confederate infantry until the arrival
of A. P. Hill's division from Harpers Ferry about 4:30 P.M., and of the
fact that, practically, it was only the devoted employment of scattered
Confederate batteries which, for a period of two hours, saved the Confederate right from being swept off the field, it seems possible that a bolder
use of his artillery by Burnside, pushing it forward with the infantry
against the piecemeal Confederate defense, might have resulted in a
clean-cut victory before A. P. Hill could have arrived. But, be that as it
may, the batteries which crossed the creek, in the absence of orders
which might have made them more effective, carried out their assigned
missions well and proved an effective barrier to further advance of the
Confederates when, toward evening, Hill's arrival enabled them to seize
the offensive and push Burnside back upon, but not away from, the last
ridge protecting the bridge.

III.

(A). A List of Confederate Battery Positions
in a Suggested Order of Priority

It need hardly be said that any classification of the batteries at Antietam,
Confederate or Federal, which assumes to list them in the order of the
importance of their services must rest entirely upon the judgment of the
individual who prepared the list. Probably no two persons would arrive at
the same results, for practically every artillery organization at Antietam
acquitted itself with distinguished courage and devotion to duty in the
situation in which it found itself.

In the following lists of the Confederate and Federal batteries the
present writer has tried merely to indicate, at the beginning, a few of the
organizations whose services, owing to their positions on the field, were

clearly conspicuous. He has designated successively, so far as practicable, batteries on different parts of the field so that, in marking positions, the guns may, from the first, be widely distributed, rather than confined closely to any one locality.

Following the batteries which are first named because of special conditions, the remaining artillery units of each army are arranged arbitrarily in an order which it is believed will insure a fairly uniform development of the program of marking over the whole field.

Batteries are designated "right," "center," or "left," according to their general locations in the line of battle of the army to which they belonged.

In introducing the priority list of Confederate batteries it seems pertinent to say a word in justification of the proposed procedure of always marking the positions of individual batteries instead of sometimes marking those of battalions or those of other groups of several batteries. It is true that at Antietam was first clearly marked a development in the tactical employment of the artillery of the Army of Northern Virginia which had already been demonstrated, but less conspicuously, at Second Manassas.

This development was in the attempted employment of large groups of guns, in the form of battalions of four or more batteries each under unified command, for definite tactical missions. The use at Second Manassas of such masses of guns as those of S. D. Lee, on the right of Jackson's line along the old railroad grade, and the two groups formed by Crutchfield behind Jackson's center and left, had proved so effective in breaking up the powerful Federal assaults that the Confederate command appears to have been induced to undertake, as far as possible, at Antietam, the consistent employment of such groups in divisional and reserve battalions. The reorganization of the artillery after the peninsular campaign had virtually provided such a battalion organization but it had been put to little practical use.

At the beginning of the Battle of Antietam such battalions, whenever they could intervene, proved far more effective than an equal number of single, scattered batteries would have proved, and a few battalions succeeded in preserving their unity, completely or partially, throughout the battle. But under the searching cross fire of the Federal artillery east of Antietam Creek and the rapid succession of tactical crises experienced by the badly outnumbered Confederate infantry, most of the battalions were eventually forced to break up so that their individual batteries could hasten to support segments of the infantry line which seemed about to be overwhelmed.

Hence, although action by battalions may have been contemplated and was sometimes accomplished, the writer believes that it would be inexpedient to attempt the marking of any battalion positions, as such. In-

stead, the marking of individual battery positions will be indicated throughout because so many batteries passed out of the direct control of their
battalion commanders and became involved in independent combats.

1. Pelham's Battery (left). Skillfully placed in probably the most effective position of any single Confederate battery on the field, it was largely
instrumental, with other batteries under Pelham's direct command, in
breaking up successive Federal attacks on Jackson's position (see end-
notes 21–24.)

2. Miller's Battery (center). Fought almost alone near the Piper buildings in defence of D. H. Hill's line after the latter had been driven from
Bloody Lane. After losses of personnel had once forced the battery to
retire, it returned with two guns and for half an hour held the enemy in
check until again driven away. Returning a third time with one more gun,
the battery, weakened by loss of men, was for some time operated with
the assistance of officers of General Longstreet's staff (notes 37–39).

3. Boyce's Battery (center). After the retirement of Miller's battery,
Boyce's pushed up nearly to the Federal line, and effectively aided D. H.
Hill's troops in repossessing the Piper buildings and forcing the enemy
back to the Bloody Lane (note 40).

4. Moody's Battery (left). Replacing three other batteries which had been
forced to retire near the Dunkard Church, one section of Moody's galloped
into a plowed field in front of the Confederate infantry and for fifteen
minutes was a decisive factor in holding the enemy in check (note 18).

5. Read's Battery (left). Was a powerful aid to McLaws's division in
repulsing, counterattacking, and driving back Sedgwick's Federal division in
the West Woods, coming to such close action in the open that it lost fourteen
men and sixteen horses in a quarter of an hour (notes 40, 41).

6. Carlton's Battery (left). Was nearly cut to pieces while giving aid,
with Read's and other batteries, to McLaws's division in driving the
Federals from the West Woods (note 32).

7. Garden's Battery (center). Together with the batteries of Squires and
others, stopped the offensive of Pleasonton's cavalry and Sykes's regular
infantry along the Boonsboro pike toward Sharpsburg. Later, with one
section of Reilly's battery, it opposed Burnside's advance across Antietam Creek, firing until so closely pressed that Garden's men saved their
guns only by running them to the rear by hand (notes 43, 46, 47).

8. Squires's Battery (center). With Garden's battery, posted on the hill
east of Sharpsburg defeated the efforts of Pleasonton's cavalry and Sykes's
infantry division to enter the town and finally, with Garnett's infantry
brigade, drove the assailants back. Later surviving elements of Squires's,
with those of other batteries, attacked Burnside's line in flank and forced
it to retire toward Burnside Bridge (notes 43, 51).

9. Jordan's Battery (left). A section of this battery, acting alone, effectively pursued Hooker's troops, retiring from their first attack, and was only stopped at last by overwhelming infantry fire. (note 11).

10. Eubank's Battery (right). With Richardson's battery for several hours opposed such a vigorous resistance to the efforts of the Federal IX Corps to cross the Burnside Bridge that the capture of the latter was delayed until after the Federal offensive on the Confederate left and center had died down. Batteries from that quarter of the field were thus enabled to go to the assistance of the Confederate right in time to save the latter from defeat, and Sharpsburg from capture.

11. Richardson's Battery (right). For several hours successfully resisted the efforts of Burnside's troops to cross the Antietam, and in cooperation with Eubank's battery retarded the Federal advance across the plateau south of Sharpsburg while other Confederate batteries came up, enabling Sharpsburg to be held until the arrival of A. P. Hill's Light Division from Harpers Ferry (note 39).

12. Bachman's Battery (right). Fought first against Hooker's advance north of the Dunkard Church, suffering heavy losses. After refitting, returned to action south of Sharpsburg and was effective in preventing the capture of Sharpsburg by Burnside's corps (notes 14, 15).

13. Woolfolk's Battery (left). In company with Parker's and Rhett's (Elliott's) batteries, also of Lee's battalion, which was the only artillery with Hood's division, fought against Hooker's second attack until its ammunition was exhausted. It then had to retire to refit, but not until after the enemy had been repulsed for the second time.[74]

14. Rhett's Battery (center). Under Lieutenant Elliott shared with Woolfolk and Parker in fighting to exhaustion against Hooker's second advance. Later went to the help of Squires and Garden and with them broke up the effort of the Federal cavalry and other troops to take possession of Sharpsburg by way of the Boonsboro pike (note 74).

15. Parker's Battery (center). With Woolfolk and Rhett aided Hood's division effectively in the morning in repulsing Hooker's second attack, and in the afternoon was instrumental in holding the hill east of Sharpsburg against Federal attacks (note 74).

16. Eshleman's Battery (right). Conducted an unflinching defense of the ford below the Burnside Bridge, repulsing all efforts of Rodman's Federal division to cross the Antietam until enfiladed by a long-range Federal battery on the other side of the stream. Compelled, then, to withdraw, Eshleman returned when A. P. Hill's division arrived in support, and again drove the enemy from the ford.[75]

17. Reilly's Battery (right). In the morning, with the rest of Frobel's battalion, opposed the hostile advance near the Dunkard Church and

fired until its rifle ammunition was exhausted. Retiring for a fresh supply, in the afternoon the battery's howitzer section with other batteries stubbornly opposed Burnside's advance toward Sharpsburg at a range of 100 yards, the guns being saved from capture only by running them to the rear by hand. The opportune arrival of Reilly's rifled section, with replenished ammunition chests, on the enemy's left, contributed materially to the eventual retirement of the latter.[76]

18. Braxton's Battery (right). Arriving with A. P. Hill's division in the afternoon, secured a position on the extreme right of Burnside's attacking line and by enfilade fire contributed powerfully to bringing about the Federal retirement from their advanced position near Sharpsburg.[77]

The remaining Confederate batteries are arbitrarily arranged in a sequence designed to bring about an even distribution of guns over the field.

19. Manly's Battery (left).
20. Maurin's Battery (center).
21. Crenshaw's Battery (right).
22. D'Aquin's Battery (left).
23. Hardaway's Battery (center).
24. McIntosh's Battery (right).
25. Brown's Battery (left).
26. Blackshear's Battery (center).
27. Pegram's Battery (right).
28. Chew's Battery (left).
29. Page's Battery (center).
30. Bondurant's Battery (center).
31. Cutshaw's Battery (right).
32. Brockenbrough's Battery (left).
33. Lane's Battery (center).
34. Read's Battery (left).
35. Moorman's Battery (center).
36. Branch's Battery (left).
37. Peyton's Battery (center).
38. Johnson's Battery (left).
39. Patterson's Battery (center).
40. Raine's Battery (left).
41. W. B. Jones's Battery (center).
42. French's Battery (left).
43. Turner's Battery (center).
44. Macon's Battery (left).
45. Thompson's Battery (center).
46. Poague's Battery (left).

47. Ross's Battery (center).
48. Hart's Battery (left).
49. Carter's Battery (center).
50. Carrington's Battery (left).
51. Wooding's Battery (center).
52. McCarthy's Battery (left).
53. Wimbish's Battery (center).
54. Dement's Battery (left).
55. Carpenter's Battery (center).
56. Balthis's Battery (left).
57. Caskie's Battery (center).

(B). A List of Federal Battery Positions in a Suggested Order of Priority

It is more difficult to designate Federal batteries which were engaged at different times in close action on the field of Antietam than it is to do so with regard to Confederate batteries. A large proportion of the Federal artillery units, although fully effective in fire, were separated throughout the action from the arena of the infantry conflict by the natural obstacle of Antietam Creek.

The Cope map shows, for example, that at the hour of 8 A.M., thirty-two Confederate batteries were in position, all of which were closely cooperating with infantry organizations of their own army. But of the forty Federal batteries in position at the same hour twenty-five were east of the Antietam, most of them in action but firing across the stream, while only fifteen were on the battlefield proper and all of these were on the Federal right, somewhere north of the Dunkard Church. Even at 4:20 P.M., when the battle was nearly over, although thirty-seven Confederate batteries were on the field, only thirty belonging to the Federals were there, of which twenty-two were still north of the Bloody Lane and the Dunkard Church, while only three were in the center, east of Sharpsburg, and five near the Burnside Bridge. There were still twenty-seven batteries east of the Antietam and most of them had been there continuously, though a few had been over to the west side and later returned.

Hence it is impracticable to propose a really balanced distribution of guns for marking Federal battery positions over the whole field. However effective may have been the fire of the batteries east of the Antietam, the positions of none of them can be marked because they stood upon ground which is not, and probably never will be, included in the national military park. Furthermore, the massing of batteries on the northern portion of the battlefield requires an even more disproportionate number of Federal positions to be marked there than is the case with Confederate positions.

As in the preceding list of Confederate batteries, there are designated at the beginning of the list of Federal batteries certain organizations which were clearly conspicuous on the field. These are followed by the remaining batteries in an order intended to develop as uniform a distribution over the field as possible. Batteries are designated "right," "center," or "left," according to their general locations in the Federal line of battle.

1. Thompson's Battery (right). Closely accompanied Hartsuff's 1st Brigade, Ricketts's Division, I Corps, in its initial advance into the cornfield north of the Dunkard Church, where, together with Matthews's battery, in an exposed position it sustained the infantry for several hours until compelled to retire for lack of ammunition (note 55).

2. Matthews's Battery (right). With Thompson's battery in the Bloody Cornfield firmly sustained the nearby Federal infantry though subjected to intense hostile musketry and artillery fire (note 55).

3. Campbell's Battery (right). Advanced with Gibbon's brigade, Doubleday's division, I Corps, into the Bloody Cornfield, where firing over the heads of its own infantry it broke up hostile counterattacks and drove back a part of Jackson's line of battle. Remaining in action with Williams's XII and Sumner's II Corps, the section under Lieutenant Stewart fought west of the Hagerstown pike, where for a time in severe fighting General Gibbon acted as a cannoneer. The battery lost thirty-eight officers and men killed and wounded and twenty-seven horses killed before retiring (note 56).

4. Edgell's Battery (right). Advancing with Hoffman's brigade, Doubleday's division, I Corps, this battery in an extremely exposed position northeast of the Dunkard Church enfiladed and drove back parts of the hostile line into the adjacent woods and neutralized enemy sharpshooters until retired to refit. The battery was again in action later in the day (note 57).

5. Monroe's Battery (right). Was in close cooperation with Edgell's battery in the engagements near the Dunkard Church and lost so many horses from the fire of enemy sharpshooters that one gun had to be withdrawn by prolonge (note 58).

6. Cothran's Battery (right). Coming on the field with the XII Corps, remained in action in front of the West Woods for six hours, most of the time closely engaged, the Confederate infantry repeatedly trying to seize the battery. While supporting Franklin's corps it repulsed one attack unaided, by firing canister (note 60).

7. Knap's Battery (right). Engaged throughout the day near the East Woods, had one of its 3-in. rifles captured while endeavoring, under

orders, to enter the woods, but replaced it with a 12-lb. howitzer taken from the enemy (note 61).

8. Tompkins's Battery (right). Supporting Sedgwick's division of Sumner's corps this battery fought for a long period near the Mumma buildings, most of the time unsupported and under enfilade fire. It broke up attempts of the enemy to capture it, was of great assistance to its own infantry, and finally retired only after expending all of its ammunition, 1,050 rounds (note 62).

9. Woodruff's Battery (right). Accompanied the advance of Sedgwick's division into the West Woods, being the only battery to do so. When Sedgwick retreated from the woods, the battery firmly resisted, and succeeded in checking, the Confederate pursuit. Being then threatened with envelopment it retired, but only when ordered to do so (note 63).

10. Graham's Battery (center). Ordered at about noon from the artillery reserve east of the Antietam to the support of Richardson's division of Sumner's corps, Graham's battery took up a position in the Federal line of battle closely fronting the Bloody Lane. Here, under concentrated fire from hostile batteries, it engaged and drove back some of the latter and also checked advances of Hill's and Anderson's infantry endeavoring to recapture the lane. While among the guns of this battery General Richardson was mortally wounded (note 69).

11. Tidball's Battery (center). Serving with Pleasonton's cavalry division, east of Antietam Creek, this battery advanced by piece under cross fire of hostile artillery, drove the Confederates from the Middle Bridge and cleared the ground for the deployment of the Federal horse artillery and its supports on the west side of the creek. Later protected Richardson's division against counterattacks by sweeping fire along the front of the division in the direction of the Bloody Lane. When Burnside's corps crossed the Antietam on the Federal left, by shifting its fire to the ground in his front Tidball's battery greatly assisted him in his advance toward Sharpsburg (note 70).

12. Robertson's Battery (center). In conjunction with Tidball's and other batteries, cleared and occupied a bridgehead west of the Antietam at the Middle Bridge, and later moved to the left of Hancock's (recently Richardson's) division, where it performed good service in breaking up Confederate offensive movements against Hancock's infantry (note 70).

13. Clark's Battery (left). Crossed the Burnside Bridge with the IX Corps and moving with the infantry across the hills against bitter resistance materially assisted Sturgis's division in advancing nearly into the streets of Sharpsburg. In the close fighting Lieutenant Baker was killed and Captain Clark four times wounded (note 73).

14. Durell's Battery (left). In company with Clark's battery went with

the advance of the IX Corps across the Burnside Bridge and in close
action with the Confederate artillery gallantly sustained the corps offensive toward Sharpsburg, later protecting its retirement toward the bridge
(note 73).

15. Cook's Battery (left). Crossed the Burnside Bridge with Willcox's
division and advanced with it toward Sharpsburg under cross fire from
the enemy. Lieutenant Coffin's section was for some time 200 yards in
front of supporting infantry and was engaged with hostile batteries at a
range of 200 yards (note 73).

The remaining Federal batteries west of the Antietam are arbitrarily
arranged in a sequence designed to bring about, as nearly as possible, an
even distribution of guns over the field.

16. Reynolds's Battery (right).
17. Hains's Battery (center).
18. C. P. Muhlenberg's Battery (left).
19. Hampton's Battery (right).
20. Gibson's Battery (center).
21. Whiting's Battery (left).
22. Hexamer's Battery (right).
23. Owen's Battery (right).
24. Simpson's Battery (right).
25. Hazard's Battery (right).
26. Cooper's Battery (right).
27. Cowan's Battery (right).
28. E. D. Muhlenberg's Battery (right).
29. Pettit's Battery (right).
30. Vanneman's Battery (right).
31. Amsden's Battery (right).
32. Martin's Battery (right).
33. Thomas's Battery (right).
34. Porter's Battery (right).
35. Ransom's Battery (right).
36. Williston's Battery (right).

Notes

1. U.S. War Department, *The War of the Rebellion: A Compilation of the Official Records of the Union and Confederate Armies* (hereafter cited as *O.R.*), ser. 1, vol. 19, pt. 1 (Washington, D.C.: GPO, 1889–90, 1897), pp. 169–80.
2. Ibid.
3. Ibid., pp. 419, 450.
4. William E. Birkhimer, *Historical Sketch of the Organization, Administration,*

Matériel, and Tactics of the Artillery, United States Army (Washington, D.C.: James J. Chapman, 1884), p. 82.

5. *O.R.*, pp. 836–37.
6. Ibid., pp. 803–10.
7. Jennings C. Wise, *The Long Arm of Lee,* vol. 1 (Lynchburg, Va.: J. P. Bell and Co., 1915), pp. 279–86.
8. *O.R.*, p. 956 (Jackson's report).
9. Ibid.
10. Wise, *The Long Arm of Lee,* p. 300.
11. *O.R.*, p. 845 (S. D. Lee's report).
12. Wise, *The Long Arm of Lee,* p. 301.
13. *O.R.*, p. 924 (Hood's report).
14. *O.R.*, p. 925 (Frobel's report).
15. Wise, *The Long Arm of Lee,* p. 300.
16. G. F. R. Henderson, *Stonewall Jackson,* vol. 2 (London: Longmans, Green, 1898), p. 247.
17. *O.R.*, p. 845 (S. D. Lee's report).
18. Ibid.
19. Henderson, *Stonewall Jackson,* p. 247.
20. Wise, *The Long Arm of Lee,* p. 301.
21. *O.R.*, p. 821 (Stuart's report).
22. Wise, *The Long Arm of Lee,* p. 301.
23. William H. Monroe, "The Battle of Antietam: A Military Study," in *Journal of the Military Service Institution* 49, no. 173 (Sept.–Oct., 1911): 258; Wise, *The Long Arm of Lee,* p. 202.
24. *O.R.*, p. 505 (Greene's report).
25. Douglas S. Freeman, *R. E. Lee,* vol. 2 (New York: Charles Scribner's Sons, 1934–35), p. 389.
26. Wise, *The Long Arm of Lee,* p. 303.
27. Ibid.
28. *O.R.*, p. 277 (Hancock's report).
29. *O.R.*, p. 1023 (D. H. Hill's report).
30. Henderson, *Stonewall Jackson,* pp. 251–52.
31. *O.R.*, p. 858 (McLaws's report).
32. Ibid.
33. Henderson, *Stonewall Jackson,* p. 254.
34. Wise, *The Long Arm of Lee,* p. 305.
35. Monroe, "The Battle of Antietam," p. 271.
36. *O.R.*, pp. 1030–31 (Carter's report).
37. Ibid., p. 849 (Walton's report).
38. Ibid., p. 840 (Longstreet's report).
39. Ibid., p. 850 (Walton's report).
40. Ibid., p. 943 (Boyce's report).
41. Ibid., p. 1024 (D. H. Hill's report).
42. Wise, *The Long Arm of Lee,* p. 308.

43. Ibid.

44. *O.R.,* pp. 845–46 (S. D. Lee's report).

45. Ibid., p. 926 (Frobel's report).

46. Ibid.

47. Wise, *The Long Arm of Lee,* p. 309.

48. *O.R.,* p. 981 (A. P. Hill's report).

49. E. A. Carman and E. B. Cope., *Map[s] of the Battlefield of Antietam,* rev. ed. (Washington, D.C., Antietam Battlefield Board, 1908), map no. 14.

50. Monroe, "The Battle of Antietam," p. 277; *O.R.,* p. 981 (A. P. Hill's report).

51. Wise, *The Long Arm of Lee,* pp. 311–12.

52. *O.R.,* p. 809, footnote.

53. Wise, *The Long Arm of Lee,* pp. 298–307.

54. *O.R.,* p. 227 (Monroe's report).

55. Ibid., p. 259 (Ricketts's report).

56. Ibid., p. 227 (Monroe's report), p. 229 (Stewart's report), pp. 248–49 (Gibbon's report); Wise, *The Long Arm of Lee,* p. 299.

57. *O.R.,* pp. 227–28 (Monroe's report), p. 236 (Hoffman's report), p. 259 (Ricketts's report).

58. Ibid., pp. 228–29 (Monroe's report).

59. Ibid., p. 259 (Ricketts's report).

60. Ibid., p. 482 (Best's report), p. 483 (Cothran's report); George B. McClellan, *McClellan's Own Story* (New York: Charles L. Webster, 1887), pp. 591–92.

61. *O.R.,* p. 477 (Williams's report), p. 482 (Best's report).

62. Ibid., p. 308 (Tompkins's report), p. 307 (Howard's report), p. 269 (Meade's report).

63. Ibid., pp. 306–307 (Howard's report), pp. 308–309 (Tompkins's report), pp. 309–10 (Woodruff's report).

64. Carman, *Map[s] of Antietam,* map no. 13.

65. Monroe, "The Battle of Antietam," p. 263.

66. Wise, *The Long Arm of Lee,* p. 304.

67. Henderson, *Stonewall Jackson,* pp. 261–62.

68. Monroe, "The Battle of Antietam," p. 257, p. 273.

69. *O.R.,* p. 343 (Graham's report); McClellan, *McClellan's Own Story,* p. 597.

70. *O.R.,* pp. 211–12 (Pleasonton's report), p. 279 (Hancock's report); Monroe, "The Battle of Antietam," pp. 274–75; McClellan, *McClellan's Own Story,* p. 597.

71. *O.R.,* pp. 443–45 (Sturgis's report), p. 447 (Nagle's report); Monroe, "The Battle of Antietam," p. 276.

72. Carman, *Map[s] of Antietam,* map no. 13.

73. *O.R.,* p. 447 (Nagle's report), p. 434 (Cook's report), p. 435 (Coffin's report).

74. Ibid., p. 846 (S. D. Lee's report).

75. Ibid., p. 850 (Walton's report).

76. Ibid., pp. 925–26 (Frobel's report).

77. Ibid., p. 981 (A. P. Hill's report).

4

Union Artillery:
Antietam, September 17, 1862
Curt Johnson and Richard C. Anderson, Jr.

Key

BLR = Breech-loading rifle
FG = Field gun
RML = Rifled muzzleloader
SBML = Smoothbore muzzleloader
12-lb. Napoleon = Model 1857 12-lb. light gun–howitzer
12-lb. Howitzer = Model 1841 12-lb. howitzer
32-lb. Howitzer = Model 1841 32-lb. howitzer
6-lb. SBML = Model 1841 6-lb. gun

Abbreviations

Note: State abbreviations are those employed by the United States Postal Service; it is not thought necessary to define them.

AOCS = Artillery Organizations of the Confederate States
(U.S. War Department; see References)
AAR = After-action report
Arty. = Artillery
Batts. = Batteries
BC = Battle casualties
Bde. = Brigade
Bn. = Battalion
Brig. Gen. = Brigadier general
Bty. = Battery
Capt. = Captain
Cav. = Cavalry
Co. = Company
Col. = Colonel
Comdg. = Commanding

Comdr. = Commander
CMIA = Captured/missing in action
CS = Confederate States
CV = *Confederate Veteran* (journal)
Div. = Division
DOW = Died of wounds
Elms. = Elements
EM = Enlisted man (men)
FG = Field gun
F.p.s. = Feet per second (muzzle velocity)
In. = Inch(es)
Inf. = Infantry
KIA = Killed in action
Lb. = Pound (-pounder)
Lt. = Lieutenant
Ltr. = Letter
Maj. = Major
MR = Muster roll(s)
MWIA = Mortally wounded in action (technically WIA)
Off. = Officer(s)
O.R. = *Official Records* (U.S. War
          Department; see References)
PFD = Present for duty
PW = Prisoner of war
Rds. = Rounds
RG = Record Group (U.S. National Archives)
Rgt. = Regiment
Rpt(s). = Report(s)
Rptd. = Reported
RMO = *Reports of Military Operations during
          the Rebellion* (Davis; see References)
SHSP = *Southern Historical Society Papers* (journal)
Str. = Strength
TBC = Total battle casualties
U/I = Unidentified
WIA = Wounded in action

Army of the Potomac

The chief of artillery of the Army of the Potomac was Col. Henry
Jackson Hunt, appointed Sept. 5, 1862 (Hunt Papers, Special Orders no.
2, container 7).

I Corps: Chief of Arty. Maj. Davis Tillson: Carman MS, 23:6 gives the total arty. complement of the corps as 46 guns, 819 men. BC were 18 KIA, 83 WIA, and 10 CMIA=111.

1st Div.:

Chief of Arty. Capt. J. Albert Monroe: Ibid. states that the 1st Div.'s arty. consisted of 4 6-gun batts. (24 guns) manned by 450 men total. BC were 12 KIA, 46 WIA, 8 CMIA=66 (*O.R.*, ser. 27:189–90).

First Bty. (Bty. A), NH Light, Lt. Frederick M. Edgell: 6 12-lb. Napoleon SBML.

The armament follows the account of J. J. (?) Piper: "The Battery had in this engagement 6 12-lb. Howitzers for guns, which are a short-range gun but good work was done with them that morning" (Studies Antietam 1894, Piper to Carman).

Barry (Hunt Papers, Barry to Hunt, p. 3) gives 4 3-in. Ordnance RML, 2 12-lb. Napoleon SBML and, crossed out, 6 12-lb. Napoleon SBML; Hunt (Hunt Papers, "Memorandum") gives both armaments but predates Barry's rpt. Marvel (Marvel 1985, p. 17) states that the bty. was reequipped with 3-in. Parrott RML after Antietam (Oct.?), citing a ltr. of Edgell to NH Adjutant General Anthony Colby of April 25, 1863, in the NH Archives.

The bty.'s return for Aug., 1862 (dated Sept. 23, 1862), lists 6 U/I field guns and a PFD strength of 2 off., 119 EM=121 (Hunt Papers, container 7). The bty. had been armed with 6 12-lb. Napoleon SBML at 2nd Manassas, where it lost a gun to Law's Bde. on the evening of Aug. 29 and was badly cut up, losing its cmdr., Capt. Gerrish (WIA, CMIA), 10 other CMIA, 2 KIA, and at least 1 WIA (*O.R.*, ser. 16:623; Marvel 1985, pp. 6–9). Its Antietam BC were 3 WIA (*O.R.*, ser. 27:189; Marvel 1985, pp. 14–15).

Bty. D, 1st RI, Capt. J. Albert Monroe: 6 12-lb. Napoleon SBML.

Barry (Hunt Papers, Barry to Hunt, p. 3) and Hunt (Hunt Papers, "Memorandum") give this armament; Hunt also has "10-lb. Parrott" crossed out. The bty. had been equipped with 6 10-lb. Parrott RML during the 2nd Manassas campaign. BC at Antietam were 3 KIA, 7 WIA, 8 CMIA=18 (*O.R.*, ser. 27:189).

Bty. L, 1st NY, Capt. John A. Reynolds: 6 3-in. Ordnance RML.

Barry (Hunt Papers, Barry to Hunt, p. 3) gives this armament, as does

Hunt (Hunt Papers, "My First Efforts," p. 2). Hunt lists the bty. under Banks's [i.e., Mansfield's XII] corps, and Barry notes that the bty. was "temporarily attached" from Banks's corps. The bty. had been with King's (Hatch's) div. in the 2nd Manassas campaign, when it was equipped with 6 10-lb. Parrott RML, but was with Banks's corps at Cedar Mountain on August 9, immediately preceding the Second Manassas campaign. Antietam BC were 5 WIA (*O.R.,* ser. 27:190).

Reynolds's return for Sept. (Hunt Papers, container 7) gives 4 off., 80 EM=84 PFD.

Bty. B, 4th U.S., Capt. Joseph B. Campbell (WIA), Lt. James Stewart: 6 12-lb. Napoleon SBML.
Barry (Hunt Papers, Barry to Hunt, p. 3) gives this armament. The bty. had "about 100 men present for duty" (Buell 1890, p. 34); BC were 9 KIA, 31 WIA=40 (*O.R.,* ser. 27:190). Stewart's return of Sept. 24, 1862, gives 1 off., 15 EM PFD, not including volunteers (Hunt Papers, container 7).

2nd Div.:
Carman (Carman MS, 23:3–4) states that the 2 4-gun batts. of the div. were "short-handed" and had just 6 off., 115 EM aggregate. BC were 3 KIA, 19 WIA, and 2 CMIA=24 (*O.R.,* ser. 27:190).

Bty. F, 1st PA Light, Capt. Ezra W. Matthews: 4 3-in. Ordnance RML.
Barry (Hunt Papers, Barry to Hunt, p. 3) and Hunt (Hunt Papers, "Memorandum," p. 8) give the armament. BC were 3 KIA, 8 WIA=11 (*O.R.,* ser. 27:190). Matthews's return of Sept. 23 gives the bty.'s EM strength as 76 (Hunt Papers, container 7).

Indpt. Bty. C, PA Light, Capt. James Thompson: 4 3-in. Ordnance RML.
Barry (Hunt Papers, Barry to Hunt, p. 3) gives the armament. Return of Thompson's bty., Sept. 24, 1862, shows PFD 1 off., 44 EM and lists 10 EM WIA (?) Sept. 17 (Hunt Papers, container 7). Thompson's rpt. (*O.R.,* ser. 107:139) gives 12 WIA, incl. 2 MWIA from the 105th NY, as the bty.'s BC at Antietam. *Official Records* (ser. 27:190) gives 11 WIA, 2 CMIA=13.

3rd Div.:
Carman (Carman MS, 23:4) gives Simpson and Cooper as 4 guns each and states that they had "3 officers each and about 16 men to a gun." He

gives Ransom as 6 guns, with 4 off., 110 EM. The div. aggregate was 14 guns, 248 off. and EM. BC were 3 KIA, 18 WIA=21 (*O.R.*, ser. 27:191).

Bty. A, 1st PA Light, Lt. John G. Simpson: 4 12-lb. Napoleon SBML.
Barry (Hunt Papers, Barry to Hunt, p. 3) and Hunt (Hunt Papers, "Memorandum," p. 8) give the armament; BC were 1 KIA, 3 WIA=4 (*O.R.*, ser. 27:191). Simpson's return of Sept. 24, 1862, gives 1 off., 89 EM=90 PFD (Hunt Papers, container 7).

Bty. B, 1st PA Light, Capt. James H. Cooper: 4 3-in. Ordnance RML.
Barry (Hunt Papers, Barry to Hunt, p. 3) and Hunt (Hunt Papers, "Memorandum," p. 8) give the armament; BC were 2 WIA (*O.R.*, ser. 27:191).

Bty. C, 5th U.S., Capt. Dunbar H. Ransom: 4 12-lb. Napoleon SBML.
Barry (Hunt Papers, Barry to Hunt, p. 3) and Hunt (Hunt Papers, "Memorandum," p. 2) give the armament; BC were 2 KIA, 13 WIA=15 (*O.R.*, ser. 27:191).

II Corps: Chief of Arty. Capt. F. N. Clark: Carman (Carman MS, 23:8–9) gives the II Corps' arty. as 7 6-gun batts. (42 pieces) manned by a total of 859 men. BC were 6 KIA, 33 WIA=39 (*O.R.*, ser. 27:192–93).

1st Div.:
Carman (Carman MS, 23:8) gives the div.'s art. as 2 6-gun batts. with 3 offs. each and 20 men/gun, aggregate 12 guns and 246 men.

Bty. B, 1st NY, Capt. Rufus D. Pettit: 6 10-lb. Parrott RML.
Armament is given in Hunt (Hunt Papers, "My First Efforts," p. 3); BC were 1 WIA on the sixteenth (*RMO*, 6:403) and 1 KIA on the seventeenth (*O.R.*, ser. 27:192).

Batts. A and C (consolidated), 4th U.S., Lt. Evan Thomas: 6 12-lb. Napoleon SBML.
Hunt (Hunt Papers, "My First Efforts," p. 3) gives the armament; BC were 3 WIA (*O.R.*, ser. 27:192).

2nd Div.:
Carman (Carman MS, 23:9) gives the div. 2 6-gun batts. with 244 men

aggregate. Tompkins had 3 off., 117 EM=120; Woodruff had 4 off., 120 EM=124.

Bty. A, 1st RI, Capt. John A. Tompkins: 6 10-lb. Parrott RML.
Hunt (Hunt Papers, "My First Efforts," p. 3) gives the bty.'s armament. BC were 4 KIA, 15 WIA=19 (*O.R.*, ser. 27:193). Tompkins stated, "Since the battle I have exchanged my Parrott guns for a new battery of 3-inch Ordnance pieces" (*RMO*, 6:401). The bty. expended 1,050 rounds during the battle. Tompkins's return of Sept. 23, 1862, gives 3 off., 106 EM PFD, total 109 (Hunt Papers, container 7). Carman states, "It is doubtful if any battery on the field did more solid and efficient work than Tompkins'" (Carman MS, 19:3).

Bty. I, 1st U.S., Lt. George A. Woodruff: 6 12-lb. Napoleon SBML.
Hunt (Hunt Papers, "My First Efforts," p. 3) provides the bty.'s armament. BC were 6 WIA (*O.R.*, ser. 27:193); see also Woodruff's AAR (Hunt Papers, container 7).

3rd Div.: None assigned.

Unattached Arty.:
Carman (Carman MS, 23:9) gives the unattached arty. as 3 6-gun batts., with 9 off. and 360 EM=369 aggregate. BC were 1 KIA, 9 WIA=10 (*O.R.*, ser. 27:193). In the listing below, the armament of each bty. is based on Hunt (Hunt Papers, "My First Efforts", p. 3).

Bty. G, 1st NY, Capt. John D. Frank: 6 12-lb. Napoleon SBML.
BC were 1 KIA, 4 WIA=5 (*O.R.*, ser. 27:193). Frank's return for Sept. (Hunt Papers, container 7) gives 5 WIA (1 DOW) and a strength of 5 off., 118 EM.

Bty. B, 1st RI, Capt. John G. Hazard: 6 12-lb. Napoleon SBML.
Hazard's return of Sept. 30 (Hunt Papers, container 7) gives his strength as 3 off., 128 EM=131 and lists no BC for Antietam.

Bty. G, 1st RI, Capt. Charles G. Owen: 6 3-in. Ordnance RML.
BC were 5 WIA (*O.R.*, ser. 27:193). Bty. G relieved Tompkins's bty. in its position on Mumma's farm. According to Reichardt (Reichardt 1865,

p. 66): "Battery G fired only a few rounds, and left the position we held for four hours and a half."

IV Corps (not engaged): Listed under Keyes's corps (Hunt Papers, Barry to Hunt, p. 6). None of these batts. was present during the battle of the seventeenth, and none appears to have incurred BC on the eighteenth, when elms. of the corps incurred a small number of BC. No personnel strength data for these batts. have been discovered.

1st Div. (Couch's Div.; attached to VI Corps):

3rd NY Bty., Capt. William Stuart: 2 12-lb. Napoleon SBML, 4 10-lb. Parrott RML.
The armament is given in Hunt (Hunt Papers, "Memorandum," p. 6).

Bty. C, 1st PA Light, Capt. Jeremiah McCarthy: 4 10-lb. Parrott RML.
Barry (Hunt Papers, Barry to Hunt, p. 6) gives the bty.'s armament.

Bty. D, 1st PA Light, Capt. Michael Hall: 4 10-lb. Parrott RML.
Barry (Hunt Papers, Barry to Hunt, p. 6) gives the bty.'s armament.

Bty. G, 2nd U.S., Lt. J. H. Butler: 4 12-lb. Napoleon SBML.
Hunt (Hunt Papers, "Memorandum," p. 1) gives the bty.'s armament.

V Corps: Carman (Carman MS, 23:13–14) gives the corps arty. as 6 batts., each of 6 guns, and each with an estimated strength of 3 off. and 115 EM. He states (Carman MS, 23:13) that only 5 of the 6 batts. were engaged and gives an aggregate engaged of 15 off., 575 EM=590. However, he notes, "All the artillery of the corps, 13 batteries, was in action" (Carman MS, 23:12). This figure includes the 7 batts. of the Arty. Reserve (for which see below). Clearly, Carman includes only the batts. of the 1st and 2nd Divs. in his estimates. It is not clear why he stated in one place that only 5 of these 6 batts. were engaged and gave a strength figure for those 5. The personnel strength figure for 6 batts. would be 18 off., 690 EM=708. BC of the arty. of the V Corps proper were 3 WIA (O.R., ser. 27:194).

1st Div.:

3rd Bty. (Bty. C), MA Light, Capt. Augustus P. Martin: 6 12-lb. Napoleon SBML.
Barry (Hunt Papers, Barry to Hunt, p. 7) gives the bty.'s armament.

Bty. C, 1st RI, Capt. Richard Waterman: 6 12-lb. Napoleon SBML.
Barry (Hunt Papers, Barry to Hunt, p. 7) gives the bty.'s armament.

Bty. D, 5th U.S., Lt. Charles E. Hazlett: 4 10-lb. Parrott RML, 2 12-lb. Napoleon SBML.
Barry (Hunt Papers, Barry to Hunt, p. 7) gives the bty.'s armament.

2nd Div.:

Batts. E and G (consolidated), 1st U.S., Lt. Alanson M. Randol: 4 12-lb. Napoleon SBML.
Barry (ibid.) gives the bty.'s armament.

Bty. I, 5th U.S., Capt. Stephen H. Weed: 4 3-in. Ordnance RML.
Hunt (Hunt Papers, "Memorandum," p. 2) gives the bty.'s armament. BC were 3 WIA (*O.R.*, ser. 27:194).

Bty. K, 5th U.S., Lt. William E. Van Reed: 4 12-lb. Napoleon SBML.
Hunt (Hunt Papers, "Memorandum," p. 2) gives the bty.'s armament.

3rd Div.:
This div. (Humphreys's) did not close on the battlefield until the eighteenth; neither of its batts. was engaged.

Bty. C, 1st NY, Capt. Almont Barnes: 2 3-in. Ordnance RML.
The bty. had lost a section (2 guns) to Trimble's bde. at Manassas Junction (night of August 26–27) and evidently had not reequipped (*O.R.*, ser. 16:402–403).
The bty.'s armament is given in Barry (Hunt Papers, Barry to Hunt, p. 7) and Hunt (Hunt Papers, "Memorandum," p. 5).

Bty. L, 1st OH, Capt. Lucius N. Robinson: 6 12-lb. Napoleon SBML.
Barry (Hunt Papers, Barry to Hunt, p. 7) gives the bty.'s armament.

Arty. Reserve: Lt. Col. William Hays.
Carman (Carman MS, 23:13–14) gives the Reserve Arty. as 7 batts., 42 guns, and about 950 personnel engaged. He includes the Reserve with the Fifth Corps arty. BC of the Reserve Arty. were 5 KIA, 5 WIA, 1 CMIA=11 (*O.R.*, ser. 27:194).

Bty. A, 1st Bn., NY Light, Lt. Bernhard Wever: 4 20-lb.
Parrott RML.
The armament of all the batts. of the 1st Bn., NY Light, are given in Hunt (Hunt Papers, "Memorandum," p. 6). BC of the bn.'s batts. are consolidated in the return (*O.R.*, ser. 27:194) and given as 1 KIA, 1 CMIA. Naisawald (Naisawald 1960, pp. 187–88) mentions a Maj. [Albert] Arndt, comdg. "1st German Battalion," as MWIA at Antietam. Arndt does not appear in any of the various orders of battle associated with Antietam but is listed as the commander of the bn. for the peninsula campaign.

Carman states, "Batteries A, B, C, and D New York Light Artillery formed a battalion under command of Maj. Albert Arndt, who was mortally wounded September 16th" (Carman MS, 11, n. 18).

Hays's AAR states that Arndt was MWIA on the sixteenth and DOW on the eighteenth (Hunt Papers, container 7).

Bty. B, 1st Bn., NY Light, Lt. Alfred von Kleiser: 4 20-lb.
Parrott RML.

Bty. C, 1st Bn., NY Light, Capt. Robert Langner: 4 20-lb.
Parrott RML.

Bty. D, 1st Bn., NY Light, Capt. Charles Kusserow: 6 32-lb.
howitzer.

5th Bty., NY Light, Capt. Elijah D. Taft: 4 20-lb. Parrott
RML.
Hunt (Hunt Papers, "Memorandum," p. 6) gives the bty.'s armament.

Bty. K, 1st U.S., Capt. William M. Graham: 6 12-lb. Napoleon
SBML.
Hunt (Hunt Papers, "Memorandum," p. 1) gives the bty.'s armament. BC were 4 KIA, 5 WIA=9. Graham rptd. expending 192 rds. (Hunt Papers, AAR, container 7).

Bty. G, 4th U.S., Lt. Marcus P. Miller: 6 12-lb. Napoleon
SBML.
Hunt (Hunt Papers, "Memorandum," p. 2) gives the bty.'s armament.

VI Corps: Carman (Carman MS, 23:15) states that the corps had 7 batts., 6 of 6 guns each and 1 of 8 guns, for a total of 44 guns, all of which were engaged. He estimates that each bty. had 3 off. (total) and 20 EM/gun and that the aggregate strength of the corps' arty. was 21 off., 880 EM=901. BC were 1 KIA, 13 WIA, 2 CMIA=16 (O.R., ser. 27:195). The armament for each bty. is given by Barry (Hunt Papers, Barry to Hunt, p. 9).

   1st Div.: Chief of Arty., Capt. Emory Upton.

   Bty. A, MD Light, Capt. John W. Wolcott: 8 3-in. Ordnance RML.
BC were 1 KIA, 11 WIA, 2 CMIA=14 (O.R., ser. 27:195). Wolcott's "List of Casualties" (Hunt Papers, container 7) gives 1 KIA, 12 WIA, 1 CMIA=14.

   1st Bty. (Bty. A), MA Light, Capt. Josiah Porter: 6 12-lb. Napoleon SBML. This bty. was not engaged (see Upton's AAR).

   1st Bty. (Bty. A), NJ Light, Capt. William Hexamer: 6 10-lb. Parrott RML.

   Bty. D, 2nd U.S., Lt. Edward B. Williston: 6 12-lb. Napoleon SBML.
Williston's BC were 2 WIA (O.R., ser. 27:195; Hunt Papers, Williston's "List of Casualties," container 7).

   2nd Div.: Chief of Arty., Capt. Romeyn B. Ayres. The batts. of the 2nd Div. did not rpt. any BC for Antietam. Barry (Hunt Papers, Barry to Hunt, p. 9) gives the armament of each bty.

   Bty. B, MD Light, Lt. Theodore J. Vanneman: 6 3-in. Ordnance RML.

   1st Bty., NY Light, Capt. Andrew Cowan: 4 3-in. Ordnance RML.

   Bty. F, 5th U.S., Lt. Leonard Martin: 4 10-lb. Parrott RML, 2 12-lb. Napoleon SBML.

IX Corps: Chief of Arty., Lt. Col. George W. Getty:
Carman states that the corps had 32 guns in action, an
evident error (Carman MS, 23:18). The personnel strength
of the corps arty. engaged was 979, according to Carman,
who did not include Whiting in his calculation (ibid., 23:16–
18); BC were 2 KIA, 14 WIA=16 (*O.R.*, ser. 27:196–98);
TBC=17 if McMullin's deserter is included.

1st Div.: Carman states that Benjamin and Cook each
had 6 guns (but see below) and that their aggregate
strength was 6 off., 240 EM=246 (Carman Papers, 23:16).
BC were 1 WIA, in Cook's bty. (*O.R.*, ser. 27:196).

*8th Bty., MA Light, Capt. Asa M. Cook: 4 12-lb. James RML
and 2 12-lb. SB howitzers.*
Cook's armament is given in Barry (Hunt Papers, Barry to Hunt, p. 8)
and Hunt (Hunt Papers, "Memorandum," p. 1). Getty's return of Sept. 22
gives Cook's strength as 4 off., 122 EM=126 (Hunt Papers, container 7).

*Bty. E, 2nd U.S., Lt. Samuel N. Benjamin: 4 20-lb. Parrott
RML.*
Benjamin's armament is given in Barry (Hunt Papers, Barry to Hunt,
p. 8) and Hunt (Hunt Papers, "Memorandum," p. 1). Getty's return of
Sept. 22, 1862, gives Benjamin's strength as 3 off., 97 EM=100 (Hunt
Papers, container 7). Benjamin's return of Oct. 1, 1862, gives his strength
that date as 3 off., 90 EM=93 (ibid.).

2nd Div.: Carman gives Clark and Durell as 6 guns each
(but see below) and an aggregate of 5 off., 236 EM=241
(Carman MS, 23:16). BC in the div.'s arty. were 2 KIA,
4 WIA=6 (*O.R.*, ser. 27:197).

*Indpt. Bty. D, PA Light, Capt. George W. Durell: 6 10-lb.
Parrott RML.*
Hunt (Hunt Papers, "Memorandum," p. 8) gives the bty.'s armament.
Durell's BC were 3 WIA (*O.R.*, ser. 27:197). Cuffel's detailed history of
the bty. gives the names of 2 men "severely wounded" (Cuffel 1900, p.
83). Durell's return of Sept. 30, 1862, gives 4 off., 116 EM=120 PFD and
notes that the bty. had "too many horses" (117); Getty's return of Sept. 22
gives Durell 4 off., 119 EM=123 PFD (Hunt Papers, container 7).
   Durell's was a crack bty. that apparently fired the rounds that produced
the explosion of the Confederate caisson depicted in the sketch in *B&L*

(Johnson and Buel, 2:647), and the "second best shot I ever saw," according to Longstreet (ibid., p. 671), which took off the front legs of D. H. Hill's white horse at a distance of 2,640 yards (Cuffel 1900, p. 78). It is fair to point out that the round fired in the second instance has been attributed to (then) Capt. Stephen H. Weed, Bty. I, 5th U.S. (ibid., n. 671).

Bty. E, 4th U.S., Capt. Joseph C. Clark, Jr. (WIA); Lt. George Dickenson: 4 10-lb. Parrott RML.

Barry (Hunt Papers, Barry to Hunt, p. 8) gives the bty.'s armament; BC were 2 KIA, 1 WIA=3 (O.R., ser. 27:197). Clark's return of Sept. 30, by Lt. Dickenson, gives 1 off., 52 EM PFD; Getty's return of Sept. 22 gives Clark 2 off., 57 EM=59 (Hunt Papers, container 7).

3rd Div.:

Carman (Carman MS, 23:17) gives Muhlenberg as 6 guns and estimates his strength as 3 off., 120 EM=123. He gives Whiting's (Bty.) Co. K, 9th NY, as 5 guns but does not calculate this co. in the arty. strength, since, in his opinion, it fought as infantry (but see below). BC of the 3rd Div. arty. were 3 WIA (O.R., ser. 27:197).

Bty. A, 5th U.S., Lt. Charles P. Muhlenberg: 6 12-lb. Napoleon SBML.

Barry (Hunt Papers, Barry to Hunt, p. 8) gives the bty.'s armament; BC were 3 WIA (O.R., ser. 27:197). Muhlenberg's return for Sept. gives the bty.'s strength as 3 off., 99 EM=102 and notes that 10 EM deserted during Sept. 8–16 (Hunt Papers, container 7).

9th NY Rgtl. Bty. (Co. K), Capt. James R. Whiting: 5 12-lb. Navy howitzers.

Carman's comment is interesting: "His [Whiting's] guns were brass navy howitzers, 12 pounders, two rifled and three smooth bores, each gun hauled by two horses, and the trail guided by a man on each side with a rope fastened to it" (Carman MS, 21:29). Despite Carman's comment that the co. was not engaged as arty. (see above), he states that it fired on Confederate skirmishers at Snavely's Ford, suppressing them (ibid., pp. 28–29).

The Rebellion Record (Moore 1864–68, 5:461–63) gives the 9th NY's strength at Antietam, minus F Co. at Plymouth, NC, as 469. Since the 8 inf. cos. engaged were 373 (Fox, cited in Carman MS, 23:17), the strength of Co. K was probably 96.

Kanawha Div.: Carman (Carman MS, 23:18) gives McMullin and Simmonds each as 6 guns and 3 off., 120 EM, for an aggregate of 12 guns, 6 off., and 240 EM. BC of the Kanawha Div. arty. were 6 WIA (*O.R.*, ser. 27:198).

1st Bty., OH Light, Capt. James R. McMullin: 6 10-lb. James RML (bronze).

Barry (Hunt Papers, Barry to Hunt, p. 8) and Hunt (Hunt Papers, "Memorandum," p. 10) give 6 3-in. Ordnance RML as the bty.'s armament, which is confirmed by McMullin's return of Oct. 1 (Hunt Papers, container 7). However, McMullin's AAR, printed in this booklet, explicitly refers to "3⁸⁰⁰ inch" guns, that is, James RMLs, so it is likely the bty. reequipped directly after Antietam. McMullin rptd. 1 KIA at Antietam (an infantryman attached from the 12th OH—see AAR), and 1 man deserted. The bty.'s strength on Oct. 1 was 3 off., 126 EM, with 40 men rptd. as a detail from the 12th OH (Hunt Papers, McMullin's return).

KY Bty., Capt. Seth J. Simmonds: 2 20-lb. Parrott RML, 3 10-lb. Parrott RML, 1 12-lb. SB howitzer (iron).

The bty.'s armament is given in Getty's return of Sept. 22, which gives Simmonds's strength as 95 EM (the number of off. is not legible) (Hunt Papers, container 7).

Barry (Hunt Papers, Barry to Hunt, p. 8) and Hunt (Hunt Papers, "Memorandum," p. 10) give the bty.'s armament as 6 10-lb. Parrott RML. However, it appears from Getty's return (above) and various rpts. that the bty. had a different armament—rather unorthodox and heterogeneous—and was not actually an "Ohio" bty., as it is sometimes designated (see below).

A rpt. of troops in the Kanawha Valley and vicinity, April, 1862 (*O.R.*, ser. 18:11), provides a list of troops by type, state, number of cos., and strength. No designation of rgts. is given. Two arty. batts., both given as Ohio batts., are listed under Brig. Gen. Jacob D. Cox's command.

Cox's rpt. to Frémont, April 5, 1862 (*O.R.*, ser. 18:46), states that the bty. was formed from the 1st KY Inf. Rgt. and consisted of:

3 10-lb. Parrott RML
2 10-lb. James RML (bronze)
1 6-lb. SBML (iron, captured from CS Gen. Henry A. Wise's command)

It also had "under his care":

2 20-lb. Parrott RML
1 6-lb. SBML (bronze)

Cox noted that the organization was understrength in men (98) and horses (50) and was not able to man all the guns of the bty. (presumably the first 6 listed above).

McClellan's rpt. of South Mountain (*O.R.*, ser. 27:49) mentions 2 20-lb. Parrott RML of Simmonds's bty. (This is obviously taken from Cox's rpt., below.)

Burnside's rpt. of Sharpsburg, dated Sept. 30, mentions Benjamin with 6 20-lb. Parrott RML. Cox's rpt., below, makes clear that this includes Simmonds's 2 guns, which were placed with Benjamin's 4, to cover the bridge.

Cox's rpt. of Sharpsburg, dated Sept. 23 (*O.R.*, ser. 27:424), states that Simmonds's 2 20-lb. Parrott RML were attached to Benjamin, ca. 0700 hrs. Sept. 17. Cox's rpt. of South Mountain, dated Sept. 20 (*O.R.*, ser. 27:458–61), states that one of Simmonds's sections with 2 20-lb. Parrott RML was in reserve. It later describes Simmonds's "advanced section" of 2 10-lb. Parrott RML being pushed forward to support McMullin's section versus Hood.

An index listing (*O.R.*, ser. 107:1, 375) notes that the final designation of the bty. was the 1st KY Bty.

From this it appears that the bty. was raised from the 1st KY Inf., probably at the time that Kentucky was attempting to maintain neutrality. To disguise the raising of troops from Kentucky (so as to appear to be respecting the state's neutrality), the bty. was probably given a fictitious designation as an Ohio bty. This may be confirmed by the fact that none of Cox's Kanawha troops are given as from Kentucky, although there must have been a Kentucky inf. rgt. (the 1st) present (*O.R*, ser. 18:11). Also, given the nature of the early conflict in that region, it is possible that the bty. was composed of Kentuckians, Ohioans, and (West) Virginians.

Regarding its armament, Getty's return accords with Cox's description of the bty. as a "mixed" bty. in *B&L* (2:652). Note that in *B&L*, Cox calls the gun run up to the [Burnside] bridge a "light howitzer . . . one we captured in West Virginia, and had been added to the battery, which was partly made up of heavy rifled Parrott guns."

If this is so, then Hunt's rpts. must reflect an imperfect understanding of an organization that was new to him.

Unattached Arty.: The unattached arty., IX Corps, did not incur any BC at Antietam.

Batts. L and M (consolidated), 3rd U.S., Capt. John Edwards, Jr.: 4 10-lb. Parrott RML.
Carman states that Edwards was not engaged (Carman MS, 23:18). The bty. was apparently detached, on the army's left flank.

The bty.'s armament is given in Hunt (Hunt Papers, "Memorandum," p. 2) and confirmed by Getty's return of Sept. 22, which gives Edwards's strength as 3 off., 94 EM=97 (Hunt Papers, container 7).

Bty. L, 2nd NY, Capt. Jacob Roemer: 6 3-in. Ordnance RML.
Carman gives Roemer 6 guns, 3 off., 120 EM (Carman MS, 23:18).

Barry (Hunt Papers, Barry to Hunt, p. 8) gives the bty.'s armament. Strength of the bty. was 4 off., 94 EM=98 (Hunt Papers, Roemer's return, Sept., 1862, container 7). This bty. was also known as the "Flushing [NY] Battery." The bty. had belonged to Sigel's corps (1st, VA), then was transferred to Banks's (2nd, VA; Mansfield's 12th, Potomac) on Sept. 8. On Sept. 16 it was assigned to the IX Corps. Roemer states (Furney 1897, p. 89) that the bty. "fired 87 rounds and suffered no casualties" at Antietam.

XII Corps: Capt. Clermont L. Best, chief of arty. (batts. not assigned to divs). Carman (Carman MS, 23:20) notes that only 4 of the corps' 7 batts. (Cothran, Bruen, Knap, and Hampton) were engaged and that the 4 batts. aggregated 22 guns and 392 men (10 off. and 382 EM). BC in the XII Corps arty. were 1 KIA, 15 WIA, and 1 CMIA=17 (*O.R.*, 27:199).

Capt. Best's "Consolidated Report" of Sept. 22, 1862 (Hunt Papers, container 7), gives the personnel strength of these 4 batts. as 14 off., 407 EM=421. The addition of 17 BC incurred Sept. 17 gives a potential total strength of 438 for the 4 batts. at Antietam on that day.

Strength of the entire XII Corps arty. on Sept. 22 was 25 off., 684 EM=709 (Hunt Papers, Best's rpt., container 7).

4th Bty., ME Light, Capt. O'Neil W. Robinson: 6 3-in. Ordnance RML.
Hunt (Hunt Papers, "My First Efforts," p. 2) gives the bty.'s armament. This armament is confirmed by Best's rpt., which gives the personnel strength of the bty. as 4 off., 100 EM=104 on Sept. 22.

6th Bty., ME Light, Capt. Freeman McGilvery: 3 12-lb. Napoleon SBML, 1 3-in. Ordnance RML.
Best's rpt. gives the bty.'s armament. Hunt (Hunt Papers, "My First

Efforts," p. 2) gives 4 12-lb. Napoleon SBML, 2 3-in. Ordnance RML. Best gives McGilvery's strength as 4 off., 81 EM=85 on Sept. 22.

Bty. M, 1st NY, Capt. George W. Cothran: 4 10-lb. Parrott RML, 2 3-in. Ordnance RML.
The bty.'s armament is given in Hunt (Hunt Papers, "My First Efforts," p. 2); BC were 6 WIA (*O.R.*, ser. 27:199; Hunt Papers, Best's AAR). Best's rpt. confirms the armament and gives the bty.'s strength on Sept. 22 as 5 off., 119 EM=124.

10th ("Excelsior") Bty., NY Light, Capt. John T. Bruen: 6 12-lb. Napoleon SBML.
Hunt (Hunt Papers, "Memorandum," p. 6; "My First Efforts," p. 2) gives the bty.'s armament. Best's rpt. confirms the armament and gives Bruen's strength on Sept. 22 as 3 off., 114 EM=117.

Indpt. Bty. E, PA Light, Capt. Joseph M. Knap: 6 10-lb. Parrott RML.
Hunt (Hunt Papers, "My First Efforts," p. 2) gives the bty.'s armament, which is confirmed by Best's rpt. BC were 1 KIA, 6 WIA, and 1 CMIA=8 (*O.R.*, ser. 27:199; Hunt Papers, Best's AAR). Best's rpt. gives Knap's strength on Sept. 22 as 3 off., 98 EM=101. Knap's surname is invariably spelled "Knapp" in documents of the period.

Indpt. Bty. F ("Pittsburg Bty."), PA Light, Capt. R. B. Hampton: 4 10-lb. Parrott RML.
Hunt (Hunt Papers, "Memorandum," p. 8) gives the bty.'s armament (confirmed by Best's rpt.); BC were 3 WIA (*O.R.*, ser. 27:199). Best's rpt. gives Hampton's strength on Sept. 22 as 3 off., 76 EM=79.

Bty. F, 4th U.S., Lt. E. D. Muhlenberg: 6 12-lb. Napoleon SBML.
Hunt (Hunt Papers, "Memorandum," p. 2) gives the bty.'s armament; this is confirmed by Best's rpt., which gives the bty.'s strength as 2 off., 96 EM=98 on Sept. 22.

Horse Arty.:
Carman (Carman MS, 23:20) gives the aggregate for the Horse Arty. as 22 guns, 12 off., and 480 EM=492. Modification of this data to account for the detachment of Chapin's section would give 20 guns, 11 off., 440 EM=451. BC were 3 KIA, 6 WIA=9 (*O.R.*, ser. 27:200).

Bty. A, 2nd U.S., Capt. J. C. Tidball: 6 3-in. Ordnance RML.
Hunt (Hunt Papers, "Memorandum," p. 1) gives the bty.'s armament.
Tidball rptd. 1 KIA, 3 WIA=4 (*O.R.*, ser. 27:200; Hunt Papers, AAR,
container 7) and that he had fired "in all about 1,200 rounds" on the
seventeenth. He complained that his superiors did not understand the
proper employment of horse arty.

Batts. B and L (consolidated), 2nd U.S., Capt. J. M.
Robertson: 4 3-in. Ordnance RML.
Hunt (Hunt Papers, "Memorandum," p. 1) gives the bty.'s armament.

Bty. M, 2nd U.S., Lt. P. C. Hains: 6 3-in. Ordnance RML.
Hunt (ibid.) gives the bty.'s armament. BC were 2 KIA, 3 WIA=5
(*O.R.*, ser. 27:200, ser. 107:138). Hains's bty. had only 4 guns at Antietam,
since 1 section (2 guns) under Lt. R. Hunter Chapin was detached,
serving with Farnsworth's Second Cav. Bde. (Hunt Papers, Hains's
AAR, Chapin's AAR).

Batts. C and G (consolidated), 3rd U.S., Capt. H. G. Gibson:
6 3-in. Ordnance RML
Hunt (Hunt Papers, "Memorandum," p. 2) gives the bty.'s armament.

Totals:
Carman's aggregate strength, with BC, for the Union arty. engaged is:

Formation	Strength	BC
I Corps	819	111
II Corps	859	39
V Corps	1,540*	14
VI Corps	901	16
IX Corps	979	16
XII Corps	392	17
Horse Arty.	492	9
Total	**5,982**	**222 (3.71%)**

*This figure includes 590 personnel of the V Corps' Artillery (5 of 6
batteries engaged) and 950 of the Reserve Artillery.

Carman's statement of the aggregate number of Union guns engaged
(301 pieces) is:

Formation	Guns Engaged
I Corps	46
II Corps	42
V Corps	36
Arty. Reserve	42
VI Corps	44
IX Corps	32 (48)
XII Corps	22
Horse Arty.	22
Total	**286 (302)**

Note: It is not entirely clear how Carman arrived at the figure of 301 Federal
guns engaged. Using his formation-by-formation totals, the aggregate engaged Union guns was 286. Using a plausible larger figure for the IX Corps,
the aggregate would be 302.

5

Confederate Artillery: Antietam, September 17, 1862

Curt Johnson and Richard C. Anderson, Jr.

Army of Northern Virginia

I n his memoir, *Fighting for the Confederacy* (Alexander 1989, p. 168), Lt. Col. E. P. Alexander noted that in the fall of 1862 there was no real "chief of artillery" for the army or for Jackson's and Longstreet's commands. At the time of Antietam, Pendleton was the so-called chief of artillery of the army, but he had effective command only of the Artillery Reserve. Reports, returns, and requisitions of the various artillery commands were filed through Pendleton as a matter of routine and convenience. Later, when the Artillery Reserve was broken up and distributed to the corps (May, 1863), Pendleton was regarded as the head of all the army's artillery.

At the time of Antietam, Col. Stapleton Crutchfield acted as de facto chief of artillery for Jackson's wing, but his role was chiefly administrative. There was no comparable "chief" under Longstreet. In the divisions, the nominal chief was the battalion commander or the ranking battery commander (usually the same person).

Longstreet's Wing:
Note: At the time of the Battle of Antietam there were no corps organizations in the Army of Northern Virginia. The corps formation was adopted just after the battle.

McLaws's Div., Cabell's Bn., Col. Henry Coalter Cabell:
Carman (Carman MS, 23:24) states, "The number of guns of McLaws' Division on the field was 19, of these but 9 were engaged, 4 of Read's Battery, 3 of Carlton's, and 2 of McCarthy's."

Manly's (A, 1st Arty. Rgt., a.k.a. Ellis Light Arty.) NC Bty.,
Capt. Basil Charles Manly: 1 3-in. Ordnance RML, 2 12-lb.
SB howitzers, 3 6-lb. SBML.
Manly's rpt. (*O.R.*, ser. 27:876) mentions 1 rifle; no other details are given. Pendleton's rpt. lists the bty. with 1 3-in. Ordnance RML and the 5 smoothbores listed above.

Carman does not list Manly's Bty. as engaged, but McLaws's rpt. (ibid., p. 862) gives Manly's BC as 4 WIA. It is assumed that Manly's guns account for 6 of the 10 unengaged pieces given by Carman. The bty. was attached to Semmes's Bde. (Pendleton 1862; Hanson 1940).

Read's (Pulaski) GA Bty., Capt. John Postell Williamson
Read: 1 10-lb. Parrott RML, 1 3-in. Ordnance RML, 1 6-lb.
SBML, 1 12-lb. SB howitzer.
Read's rpt. (*O.R.*, ser. 27:866) mentions 2 rifles, 1 of which was a 3-in. Ordnance RML that went out of action with a broken axle before the bty. opened fire. No other guns are mentioned. Pendleton's rpt. lists the second rifle as a 10-lb. Parrott RML and also lists 1 6-lb. SBML. On Sept. 22 Read requested that his bty. be refitted. At that time he described it as consisting of 1 rifle, 1 howitzer, and 2 guns that had been disabled at Sharpsburg (*O.R.*, ser. 28:620).

McLaws's rpt. (*O.R.*, ser. 27:861–62) gives Read's engaged strength as 4 off., 74 EM=78; BC were 4 KIA, 10 WIA=14. Read states that his BC were incurred during the morning of Sept. 17 (ibid., p. 866). The bty. was attached to Kershaw's Bde. (Pendleton 1862; Hanson 1940).

Macon's (Richmond "Fayette") VA Bty., Lt. William Izard
Clopton: 2 10-lb. Parrott RML, 4 6-lb. SBML.
The bty. was named in honor of the Marquis de Lafayette, on the occasion of his visit to the United States (1824–25).

Capt. Miles C. Macon, bty. comdr., was on detached duty at Bolivar Heights, near Harpers Ferry, with the bty.'s 2 10-lb. Parrott RML. Lt. Clopton commanded the bty. at Crampton's Gap and at Antietam (Chamberlayne 1883, pp. 4, 8). It is assumed that the 4 6-lb. SBML may account for the remaining 4 unengaged pieces given by Carman (Pendleton 1862).

Carlton's (Troup) GA Bty., Capt. Henry H. Carlton: 2 10-lb.
Parrott RML, 1 12-lb. SB howitzer, 2 6-lb. SBML.
McLaws's rpt. (*O.R.*, ser. 27:861–62) gives BC of 1 KIA, 8 WIA=9. If Carman's count of 3 guns is correct, then it appears likely that the 2 6-lb. SBML were left behind at Leesburg. Carlton's strength was just 1 off.

and 26 EM=27 (Carman MS, 23:23). The bty. was attached to Cobb's Bde. (Pendleton 1862).

McCarthy's (1st Co., Richmond Howitzers) VA Bty., Capt. Edward S. McCarthy: 2 10-lb. Parrott RML, 2 6-lb. SBML.
McLaws's rpt. (*O.R.*, ser. 27:861–62) gives 1 off., 32 EM=33 engaged; BC were 1 KIA, 1 WIA=2. If Carman's count of 2 guns is accurate, then it appears likely that the 2 6-lb. SBML were left behind at Leesburg. The bty. was attached to Barksdale's bde. (Pendleton 1862; Hanson 1940).

R. H. Anderson's Div., Saunders's Bn., Maj. John Selden Saunders:
Carman (Carman MS, 23:24) gives the strength of Saunders's Bn. as 328 aggregate and 16 guns. Evidently, this does not include Chapman's Bty., attached to Featherston's Bde. BC are given as 5 KIA, 11 WIA=16 (Huger: 1 KIA, 2 WIA=3 [Porter's *History of Norfolk County*]; Moorman: 1 KIA, 7 WIA=8; Grimes: 3 KIA, 2 WIA=5 [Carman MS, 24:3–4]).

Maurin's (Donaldsonville) LA Bty., Capt. Victor Maurin: 2 10-lb. Parrott RML, 1 3-in. Ordnance RML, 3 6-lb. SBML.
Maurin's rpt. (*O.R.*, ser. 27:847) mentions 2 10-lb. Parrott RML, 1 3-in. Ordnance RML, and an unspecified number of 6-lb. SBML. Pendleton's rpt. agrees and gives the number of 6-lb. SBML as 3. This armament is confirmed by correspondence of Eugene H. Levy with Carman (Carman MS, ltr. of March 17, 1900, container 3). The bty. was assigned to Pryor's Bde. on Aug. 18, 1862 (Owen 1885, p. 100; see also Carman MS, Levy to Carman, April 21, 1900). The bty. was positioned on the right of the 4 batts. of Saunders's Bn. "Our guns were a little to the right of the barn and in *advance* of R. H. Anderson's [Division] until the division advanced through the cornfield and orchard towards Bloody Lane" (ibid.). "Carter's Virginia battery came in on our left" (Carman MS, Levy to Carman, March 3, 1900).

Maurin's BC in the action near Shepherdstown (Sept. 19) were 1 KIA, 2 WIA=3 (*O.R.*, ser. 27:838; Pendleton 1862; Alexander 1989).

Huger's (Norfolk) VA Bty., Capt. Frank Huger; Lt. C. R. Phelps: 1 10-lb. Parrott RML, 1 3-in. Ordnance RML, 2 6-lb. SBML.
The bty. was attached to Mahone's Bde. (Pendleton 1862).

*Moorman's (Lynchburg) VA Bty., Capt. Marcellus Newton
Moorman: 2 10-lb. Parrott RML, 1 U/I.*
Moorman's rpt. (*O.R.*, ser. 27:847) states that he lost 1 10-lb. Parrott
RML damaged and later removed by unknown parties (probably by
Alexander's Ordnance train) during the battle (Alexander 1989).

*Grimes's (Portsmouth) VA Bty., Capt. Cary F. Grimes
[MWIA], Lt. John H. Thompson: 1 10-lb. Parrott RML,
2 12-lb. SB Naval howitzers.*
The bty. was in action near Piper's stone barn, where Grimes was MWIA
(see Thompson, *SHSP* 34:151–53). It was disbanded Oct. 4, 1862 (Special Orders no. 209, ANV [O.R., 28:652–654).

*Chapman's (Monroe "Dixie") VA Bty., Capt. William Henry
Chapman: 1 3-in. Ordnance RML, 1 12-lb. Napoleon SBML.*
Although sometimes listed as "unattached," the bty. was associated with
Longstreet's command and assigned to Featherston's Bde. on Aug. 18,
1862 (Owen 1885, p. 100; see also Featherston's rpt. of Second Manassas,
O.R., ser. 16:604; and Wise 1959, pp. 204, 257, 283).
     At Antietam, the bty. appears to have been temporarily attached to
Kershaw's Bde. as of Sept. 7 (see Moore 1989, p. 93). On Oct. 2 the bty.
resumed its attachment to Featherston's Bde. (*O.R.*, ser. 28:649). It was
noted as present but not engaged by Carman. The bty. lost 1 WIA, 1
CMIA=2 at Boteler's Ford (Moore 1989, p. 95). It was disbanded Oct. 4,
1862 (Special Orders no. 209, ANV [*O.R.*, ser. 28:652–54]).

D. R. Jones's Div.:

*Brown's (Wise Arty.) VA Bty., Capt. James S. Brown [WIA]:
4 U/I.*
Carman (Carman MS, 23:26) gives a strength of 3 off., 78 EM=81 and 4
guns; BC are given as 1 KIA, 4 WIA, 1 CMIA=6 (ibid., 24:4, citing
muster roll of Oct. 31, 1862). The bty. was assigned to Anderson's Bde.
on Aug. 18, 1862 (Owen 1885, p. 100); it was disbanded Oct. 4, 1862
(Special Orders no. 209, ANV [*O.R.*, ser. 28:652–54]).

Walker's Div.:
Carman (Carman MS, 23:27) states that Walker's 2 batts. aggregated 230
men and 12 guns; the only BC were incurred by Branch's Bty., which lost
2 KIA, 13 WIA=15 (ibid., 24:5, citing muster roll of Oct. 31, 1862).

*French's (Stafford) VA Bty., Capt. Thomas B. French: 3
10-lb. Parrott RML, 3 12-lb. SB howitzers.*
The bty. was attached to Walker's (Manning's) Bde. (Pendleton 1862;
Hanson 1940).

*Branch's (Petersburg) VA Bty., Capt. James Read Branch:
1 10-lb. Parrott RML, 2 3-in. Ordnance RML, 3 12-lb. SB
howitzers.*
The bty. was attached to Ransom's Bde. (Pendleton 1862; Hanson 1940).

**Hood's Div., Frobel's Bn., Maj. Bushrod Washington
Frobel:**
Carman (Carman MS, 23:28) gives Frobel's Bn. as 8 off., 296 men=304
and 18 guns (but see below); BC were 4 KIA, 19 WIA=23 (Bachman: 2
KIA, 2 WIA–4; Garden: 9 WIA; Reilly: 2 KIA, 8 WIA=10 [ibid., 24:5]).
However, Garden's Bty. rptd. 12 BC (see below). Also, it appears that the
bn. had 16 guns (Pendleton 1862; Hanson 1940; *O.R.,* ser. 27:925–26,
Frobel's report).

*Bachman's (Charleston "German") SC Bty., Capt. William K.
Bachman: 4 12-lb. Napoleon SBML, 2 12-lb. Blakely RML
(Brooks 1912, pp. 279–80).*

*Garden's (Palmetto) SC Bty., Capt. Hugh R. Garden: 2 12-lb.
SB howitzers, 2 6-lb. SBML.*
Carman (Carman MS, 21:40) uses the terminology "Garden's South
Carolina battery of 12-pounders."
　　The Record of Events on the MR of Garden's Bty. for Sept., 1862,
states that the bty. was "severely engaged" at Antietam and lost 1 lt.
MWIA, 11 EM WIA=12, plus 9 horses KIA and 5 horses WIA (RG 109,
microcopy 861, roll 44).

*Reilly's (D, 1st Arty. Rgt., a.k.a. Rowan Arty.) NC Bty., Capt.
James Reilly: 2 10-lb. Parrott RML, 2 3-in. Ordnance RML,
2 24-lb. SB howitzers.*

Evans's Indpt. Bde:

*Boyce's (Macbeth) SC Bty., Capt. Robert Boyce: 6 U/I (O.R.,
ser. 16:639); Carman gives 3 off., 112 EM=115 and 6 guns
(Carman MS, 23:28) and BC of 2 KIA, 17 WIA=19 (ibid.,
24:5). BC are reported in O.R. (ser. 27:944).*
The bty. was assigned to Evans's Bde. on Aug. 18, 1862 (Owen 1885,
p. 100).

Washington (LA) Arty., Col. James Burdge Walton:
Carman (Carman MS, 23:28–29) gives the Washington arty. as 4 4-gun
batts. (16 guns) and 15 off., 263 EM aggregate; BC were 4 KIA, 28 WIA,
2 CMIA=34 (ibid., 24:6). BC given for 3 cos. (1st–3rd) in the Richmond
(VA) *Daily Dispatch* (Sept. 26, 1862) are 4 KIA, 27 WIA, 2 CMIA=33, 1
less than given by *O.R.* and Carman for 4 cos. (see below). Other sources
are Pendleton 1862; Hanson 1940; *O.R.,* ser. 27:847, Walton's rpt.

Squires's (1st Co.) Bty., Capt. Charles Winder Squires: 2 3-in.
Ordnance RML, 2 10-lb. Parrott RML. BC were 1 KIA, 12
WIA=13 (Richmond Daily Dispatch, Sept. 26, 1862).
The bty. was assigned to the Reserve Arty. of Longstreet's Wing on Aug.
18, 1862 (Owen 1885, p. 100).

Richardson's (2nd Co.) Bty., Capt. John B. Richardson: 2 12-
lb. Napoleon SBML, 2 12-lb. SB howitzers. BC were 1 KIA, 5
WIA=6 (Richmond Daily Dispatch, Sept. 26, 1862).
The bty. was assigned to Toombs's Bde. on Aug. 18, 1862 (Owen 1885,
p. 100).

Miller's (3rd Co.) Bty., Capt. M. B. Miller: 4 12-lb. Napoleon
SBML. BC were 2 KIA, 10 WIA, 2 CMIA=14 (Richmond
Daily Dispatch, Sept. 26, 1862). A nominal list in the
Charleston (SC) Daily Courier (Sept. 29, 1862, p. 4) gives BC
of the 3rd Co. as 2 KIA, 11 WIA=13 and makes no mention of
CMIA.
Miller's Co. had a caisson exploded by an enemy shell and was conspic-
uous in the defense of the Confederate center, suffering severely. Gen.
Longstreet and members of his staff helped to man the bty. at the crisis of
the battle.
    The bty. was assigned to the Reserve Arty. of Longstreet's Wing on
Aug. 18, 1862 (Owen 1885, p. 100).

Eshleman's (4th Co.) Bty., Capt. Benjamin Franklin
Eshleman: 2 12-lb. SB howitzers, 2 6-lb. SBML. No BC are
reported for the 4th Co.
The bty. was assigned to Pickett's Bde. on Aug. 18, 1862 (Owen 1885,
p. 100).

S. D. Lee's Bn., Col. Stephen Dill Lee:
S. D. Lee's rpt. (*O.R.,* ser. 27:844–45) mentions Parker (2 rifles),
Rhett (2 rifles, 2 howitzers), Jordan (1 rifle, 2 other guns), Moody (4

guns), Eubank (4 guns), and Woolfolk (no number given). Also, Lee mentions a 2-gun section commanded by a Lt. Maddox from one of Cutts's batts. as having been attached to his bn. during the day. Pendleton's rpt. lists the following:

Parker: 2 3-in. Ordnance RML, 2 12-lb. SBML howitzers.
Rhett: 2 20-lb. and 2 10-lb. Parrott RML. (It is likely that the 2 20-lb. Parrott RML in Rhett's Bty. were obtained from Harpers Ferry and were issued after the battle to replace the 2 howitzers mentioned in S. D. Lee's rpt.) "Report of Guns Captured at Harper's [*sic*] Ferry" (*O.R.,* ser. 27:548) lists 4 20-lb. Parrott RML. These were probably issued to Rhett's and Poague's batteries in late Sept.–Nov., 1862.
Jordan: 2 3-in. Ordnance RML, 1 12-lb. SBML howitzer, 1 6-lb. SBML.
Moody: 2 3-in. Ordnance RML, 2 24-lb. SBML howitzers. (Moody's initial position was in support of D. H. Hill in the center.)
Eubank: 1 3-in. Ordnance RML, 1 12-lb. SBML howitzer, 1 6-lb. SBML.
Woolfolk: not listed.

Lt. Thomas A. Maddox's section: This section was from Blackshear's Bty., Cutts's Bn. (*O.R.,* ser. 28:649), and may have been deployed between the Hagerstown Pike and Smoketown Road on the morning of Sept. 17. Barnwell's rpt. gives Maddox 1 10-lb. Parrott RML (*O.R.,* ser. 27:837–38). In the arty. reorganization of Oct. 4, 1862, Maddox's section was assigned to Milledge's GA Bty. Barnwell (ibid.) gives Milledge 4 3-in. RML and 1 12-lb. SB howitzer. Pendleton's rpt. gives Milledge 1 10-lb. Parrott RML, 3 3-in. RML, 1 Hotchkiss RML, and 1 James RML. It is assumed that the Parrott RML was from Maddox's section. The James RML may have been one of the pieces captured at Harpers Ferry.

Carman (Carman MS, 23:28) gives Lee's strength as 18 off., 300 EM=318 and 24 guns; BC were 10 KIA, 75 WIA=85 (ibid., 24:6). The Richmond *Daily Dispatch* (Sept. 30, 1862) states that the battalion lost about 80 out of 300. The Charleston (SC) *Daily Courier* (Oct. 9, 1862, p. 4) states that Lee's command lost 19 KIA, 75 WIA=94 and 56 horses. S. D. Lee, in "Three Personal Incidents of the Battle of Antietam" (Jedediah Hotchkiss Papers, container 56, Library of Congress, Manuscript Division), gives details of the battalion's fight.

Woolfolk's (Ashland) VA Bty., Capt. Pichegru Woolfolk, Jr.:
2 10-lb. Parrott RML, 1 12-lb. SB howitzer (iron).
Attached: 1 section, Fleet's (Middlesex) VA Bty.: 1 6-lb. SBML (*CV* 3:131).

Jordan's (Bedford) VA Bty., Capt. Tyler Calhoun Jordan:
1 3-in. Ordnance RML, 1 10-lb. Parrott RML, 1 12-lb. SB
howitzer, 1 6-lb. SBML.
Graves (Graves 1903, p. 24) gives BC of 1 KIA, 2 WIA=3.

Elliott's (Rhett's, a.k.a. Brooks Arty.) SC Bty., Lt. William
Elliott: 2 10-lb. Parrott RML, 2 12-lb. SB howitzers.

Eubank's ("Bath") VA Bty., Capt. John L. Eubank: 1 3-in.
Ordnance RML, 1 U/I RML, 1 12-lb. SB howitzer, 1 6-lb.
SBML.

Moody's (Madison) LA Bty., Capt. George V. Moody: 2 3-in.
Ordnance RML, 2 24-lb. SB howitzers.
The Richmond Whig (Oct. 20, 1862, p. 2, column 5) reported Moody's
BC as 4 KIA, 24 WIA=28.

Parker's (Richmond) VA Bty., Capt. William Watts Parker:
2 3-in. Ordnance RML, 2 12-lb. SB howitzers.
BC of Parker's bty. were 3 KIA, 18 WIA=21, according to the Richmond
Dispatch (Sept. 26, 1862, p. 2, column 4).

Jackson's Wing:

Ewell's Div., Courtney's Bn., Maj. Alfred Ranson
Courtney:
Krick (Krick 1991, p. 102) comments: "Relieved of A.N.Va. duty, at his
own request. . . . He had been court-martialed for dereliction of duty at
Sharpsburg, having failed to go into action with the batteries, and found
guilty on most counts."

Carman calculated Courtney's 4 batts. at 15 guns, served by 223
officers and EM (Carman MS, 23:30). Carman did not place Latimer's
section (see below) on the field but gave Dement's Bty. as engaged (ibid.,
11:46).

D'Aquin's (Louisiana Guard) LA Bty., Capt. Louis E.
D'Aquin: 1 10-lb. Parrott RML, 2 3-in. Ordnance RML.
D'Aquin's BC were reported with those of Hays's Bde., to which it was
attached, and were 1 KIA, 8 WIA=9 (*O.R.*, ser. 27:974; Pendleton 1862;
Hanson 1940).

Johnson's (Bedford) VA Bty., Capt. John R. Johnson: 3 U/I guns (either 2 12-lb. SB howitzers and 1 6-lb. SBML or 1 12-lb. SB howitzer and 2 6-lb. SBML).

Johnson's Bty. had 108 men at the end of Aug., 1862, and 104 men at the end of Sept., 1862 (Moore 1990, p. 132). Its Antietam BC were reported with those of Trimble's Bde., to which it was attached, and were 1 KIA, 10 WIA=11 (*O.R.*, ser. 27:974). The bty. was disbanded Oct. 4, 1862 (Special Orders no. 209, ANV [*O.R.*, ser. 28:652–54; Hanson 1940; Moore 1990, pp. 122, 125]).

Garber's (Balthis's Staunton) VA Bty., Lt. Asher W. Garber: 2 6-lb. SBML.

Crutchfield's rpt. (*O.R.*, ser. 27:963–64) mentions that Balthis's Bty. was to receive 2 Napoleons. Pendleton's rpt. shows that Balthis had 2 6-lb. SBML. Crutchfield's rpt. (ibid., pp. 962–63) makes no mention of Balthis's Bty. but states that the batts. left behind at Harpers Ferry were Brown's, Latimer's, and Dement's. Early's rpt. (ibid., pp. 965–75) specifically states that Balthis's Bty. was commanded by Lt. A. W. Garber and was at Harpers Ferry with the div. on Sept. 14–16. Early then states that only Brockenbrough's and D'Aquin's batts. accompanied the div. to Sharpsburg.

However, many accounts of the battle attribute the first arty. shot fired on Sept. 17 to Lt. Garber, and the Record of Events on the MR of the bty. for Oct. 31, 1862, outlines the bty.'s early employment and hard service in the battle, stating that it was attached to Lawton's Bde., lost 2 EM WIA, and had 1 caisson disabled (RG 109, microcopy 861, roll 64; also, Carman MS, 24:7).

Latimer's (Courtney) VA Bty., Capt. Joseph White Latimer: 2 3-in. Ordnance RML.

The bty. had 1 section only, equipped with guns captured at Harpers Ferry; it arrived in the late afternoon Sept. 17 according to Crutchfield's rpt. (*O.R.*, ser. 27:964).

A. P. Hill's Div., Walker's Bn., Maj. Reuben Lindsay Walker:

Carman (Carman MS, 11:49) lists the 4 batts. below, plus Davidson's. However, he gives the aggregate strength of these 4 batts. as 18 guns and 337 off. and EM (ibid., 23:30). BC were 4 KIA, 9 WIA=13 (ibid., 24:8).

Crenshaw's (Richmond) VA Bty., Capt. William G. Crenshaw: 1 12-lb. Napoleon SBML., 1 12-lb. SB howitzer, 2 6-lb. SBML.

Carman (ibid.) gives Crenshaw's BC as 1 KIA, 3 WIA=4. Carmichael

(Carmichael 1990, p. 97) gives 1 KIA, 4 WIA=5. Young and Ellett (Young and Ellett 1903, p. 279) give 3 WIA (1 MWIA).

Braxton's (Fredericksburg) VA Bty., Capt. Carter Moore Braxton: 2 3-in. Ordnance RML, 4 6-lb. SBML.
Carman (Carman MS, 24:8) gives Braxton's BC as 1 KIA, 2 WIA (est.). Krick (Krick 1986, p. 34) states that the bty. had no BC at Antietam. Its BC at Boteler's Ford were 1 KIA, 2 WIA, 1 CMIA=4 (ibid., pp. 34–35).

McIntosh's (Pee Dee) SC Bty., Capt. David Gregg McIntosh: 1 10-lb. Parrott RML, 1 3-in. Ordnance RML, 1 12-lb. Napoleon SBML, 1 12-lb. SB howitzer.
Carman (Carman MS, 24:8) gives McIntosh's BC as 1 KIA, 2 WIA.

Pegram's (Richmond "Purcell") VA Bty., Capt. William Johnson Pegram (WIA): 2 10-lb. Parrott RML, 2 12-lb. Napoleon SBML.
Carman (Carman MS, 24:8) estimates Pegram's BC as 1 KIA, 2 WIA. However, Carmichael (Carmichael 1990, p. 31) states that the only BC in the Purcell Bty. was Willy Pegram, who was struck in the head by a shell fragment and WIA at the close of the battle. These statements are contradicted by the Record of Events for Sept.–Oct., 1862, on the MR of the bty. for Oct. 31, 1862 (?), which gives its Antietam BC as 1 EM KIA, 13 WIA=14, plus 10 horses KIA (RG 109, microcopy 861, roll 64).

This MR also indicates that the bty. had 6 guns, but it's possible only 4 were brought along on this campaign (a detachment of the bty., without arty. guns, was left at Harpers Ferry).

Jackson's Div., Shumaker's Bn., Maj. Lindsay Mayo Shumaker:
Carman (Carman MS, 11:52) gives Shumaker only 5 batts. engaged: Carpenter, Brockenbrough, Wooding, Raine, and Poague. He gives the strength of these batts. as 21 guns, 15 off., and 295 EM=310 (ibid., 23:31). However, J. R. Jones's rpt. (*O.R.*, ser. 27:1008) gives the batts. engaged as Poague, Carpenter, Brockenbrough, Raine, Caskie, and Wooding. Note that Carman's count of 21 guns matches the number given for the 7 batts. below (*O.R.*, ser. 27:964, Shumaker's report; Hanson 1940).

Carpenter's (Alleghany) VA Bty., Capt. Joseph Carpenter: 1 3-in. Ordnance RML, 1 10-lb. Parrott RML, 1 12-lb. Napoleon SBML.
Carman (Carman Papers, 24:11) estimated Carpenter's BC as 1 KIA, 9

WIA=10. Bohannon (Bohannon 1990, p. 25) gives the bty.'s BC as 5 WIA; this figure is confirmed by the Record of Events on the bty.'s MR for Nov. 1, 1862, covering the period Apr. 30–Nov. 1, 1862 (RG 109, microcopy 861, roll 64). The bty. was attached to the Stonewall Bde. (Fonerden 1911).

In Studies Antietam, box 2, Carman gives the bty.'s armament as 2 3-in. Ordnance RML, 2 12-lb. Napoleon SBML.

Cutshaw's (Winchester) VA Bty., Capt. Wilfred Emory Cutshaw: 1 or 2 3-in. Ordnance RML, 2 12-lb. SB howitzers.

Bde. attachment unknown, but the bty. was attached, along with Caskie's, to an unidentified bde. On Sept. 26, 1862, the bty. was merged with Carpenter's under Special Orders no. 201, ANV (*O.R.*, ser. 28:629).

Brockenbrough's (2nd Baltimore) MD Bty., Capt. John Bowyer Brockenbrough: 1 3-in. Ordnance RML, 1 Blakely RML, 1 10-lb. Parrott RML, 1 12-lb. SB howitzer.

Brockenbrough's BC were 8 WIA (Carman MS, 24:11). The bty. was attached to Starke's Bde. Carman (Studies Antietam, box 2) gives an armament of 1 3-in. Ordnance RML, 2 Blakely RML, and 1 12-lb. SB howitzer.

Wooding's (Danville) VA Bty., Capt. George Washington Wooding: 1 10-lb. Parrott RML, 1 3-in. Ordnance RML.

Carman (Carman MS, 24:11) gives Wooding's BC as 2 KIA, 3 WIA=5. Moore (Moore 1989, p. 22) gives the bty.'s effective strength as 64 and gives its BC as 1 KIA, 13 WIA, and 1 CMIA (deserted)=15. At Martinsburg, after Antietam, it had 1 10-lb. Parrott RML, 1 3-in. Ordnance RML, and 2 6-lb. SBML (ibid., p. 24).

Carman (Studies Antietam, box 2) gives Wooding's armament at Antietam as 2 10-lb. Parrott RML, 1 3-in. Ordnance RML, and 1 12-lb. Napoleon SBML.

Raine's (Lee) VA Bty., Capt. Charles J. Raine: 2 3-in. Ordnance RML, 2 12-lb. SB howitzers.

Raine told Carman that he had 2 12-lb. howitzers and 2 rifles and that the howitzers were "no good" and ordered to the rear (Studies Antietam, box 2). Raine's BC were 5 WIA (Carman MS, 24:11, citing muster roll of Oct. 31, 1862; Studies Antietam, box 2). The bty. was attached to Starke's Bde.

Poague's (Rockbridge) VA Bty., Capt. William Thomas Poague: 2 10-lb. Parrott RML, 1 12-lb. Napoleon SBML.

Poague's rpt. (*O.R.*, ser. 27:1009) mentions 2 10-lb. Parrott RML and 1 12-lb. Napoleon SBML. His memoir (Poague 1957, p. 45) states that the bty. had 3 guns only in action at Sharpsburg. One 6-lb. SBML was detached "elsewhere," initially to Martinsburg and later to Williamsport, along with elements of Brown's Reserve Arty Bn. (Watson's 2nd Howitzers, commanded by a Lt. Jones, and a section of Hupp's Salem Arty., according to Stuart's rpt. [*O.R.*, ser. 27:820]) and the 2nd and 10th VA Inf. rgts. Pendleton's rpt. gives Poague 2 20-lb. and 2 10-lb. Parrott RML. Note, however, that the account in *SHSP* 23:141–42 states that toward the end of Sept., the bty. "turned in to the Ordnance Department one brass six-pounder; exchanged Napoleon gun for a ten-pound parrat [*sic*], and received two twenty-pounder parrot [*sic*] guns."

Poague's BC were 6 WIA (Carman MS, 24:11; *SHSP* 23:141). The bty. was attached to the Stonewall Bde.

Caskie's (Richmond "Hampden") VA Bty., Capt. William Henderson Caskie: 1 10-lb. Parrott RML.

It is likely that 3 6-lb. SBML not listed above but listed in Pendleton's rpt. were "absent," as were those of the 7 batts. rptd. by Shumaker. The bty. was attached, along with Cutshaw's Bty., to an unidentified bde. (Pendleton 1862, not reported by Shumaker).

D. H. Hill's Div., Pierson's Bn., Maj. Scipio Francis Pierson:

Wise (Wise 1959, p. 303) gives Pierson's Bn. as 16 guns. *CV* (26:72) gives 5 batts. and 21 guns (it is likely that the fifth bty. and the 5 additional guns were in G. W. Nelson's [Hanover] VA Bty., which did not cross into Maryland). Carman (Carman MS, 23:34) gives 4 batteries, 21 guns, 11 off., 335 EM=346; BC were 50 altogether (ibid., 24:9).

Hardaway's AL Bty., Capt. Robert Archelaus Hardaway: 2 3-in. Ordnance RML, 1 12-lb. Whitworth BLR.

Carman states (Studies Antietam, box 2) that Lt. John W. Tullis commanded the bty. at Antietam.

Hardaway's BC were 9 WIA (Carman MS, 24:9; Pendleton 1862; Hanson 1940).

Bondurant's (Jeff Davis) AL Bty., Capt. James William Bondurant: 3 3-in. Ordnance RML, 1 12-lb. Napoleon SBML.

Bondurant's BC were 1 KIA, 8 WIA=9 (Carman MS, 24:9). Carman notes that Bondurant went into action about noon near Piper's house and had 2 guns only in action. Besides the loss of a caisson, "one of the two pieces was dismounted and several men were killed and wounded" (Carman Papers, Carman synopsizing a ltr. from John Purifoy, container 3).

The bty.'s armament is given in a ltr. from John Purifoy to Carman (Carman Papers, Aug. 7, 1900, container 3).

Jones's (Peninsula) VA Bty., Capt. William B. Jones: 4 U/I.
Jones's BC were 1 KIA, 25 WIA=26 (Carman MS, 24:9). Wise (Wise 1959, p. 322) states that the bty.'s loss was "fully 50 per cent of its strength."

Carter's (King William) VA Bty., Capt. Thomas Henry Carter:
2 12-lb. SB howitzers, 2 6-lb. SBML, 1 10-lb. Parrott RML.
Carter's rpt. (*O.R.*, ser. 27:1030) gives 2 howitzers, 2 6-lb. SBML, and 1 Parrott; this agrees with Pendleton's rpt.

Carter's BC were 1 KIA, 3 WIA, and 1 CMIA=5 (Carman MS, 24:9). "Roster of King William Artillery" (*SHSP* 24:156–57) gives the names of 2 KIA at Antietam. Macaluso (Macaluso 1991, p. 29) gives 2 KIA, 3 WIA, 1 PW=6. The bty. was attached to Rodes's Bde. (Pendleton 1862; Hanson 1940).

General Reserve Arty., Brig. Gen. William N. Pendleton:
The General Reserve Arty., Army of Northern Virginia,
consisted of 5 bns. (Cutts's, H. P. Jones's, Brown's,
Nelson's, and S. D. Lee's)—25 batteries. However, Brown's
and Nelson's bns. were on the Virginia side of the Potomac
on the seventeenth and not engaged in the Battle of
Antietam. The bns. engaged were those of S. D. Lee, Cutts,
and H. P. Jones.

Cutts's (Sumter) GA Arty. Bn., Lt. Col. Allen Sherrod Cutts:
The strength and deployment of Cutts's Bn. in the battle is something of a mystery. In the confusion of the withdrawal from South Mountain on September 14–15, Cutts was mistakenly left behind in his bivouac near Boonsboro. Realizing that he had suddenly (and inadvertently) become the rear guard of the army, Cutts hurriedly started moving toward Sharpsburg on the Williamsport road with his own 4 batts. (23 guns), as well as Bondurant's Bty. (4 guns) and Lloyd's Bty. (3 guns). Skirting the advancing Union army, Cutts rejoined the army at Sharpsburg, marching in on the Hagerstown pike. At Sharpsburg, Bondurant rejoined Pierson's Bn., while Lloyd remained with Cutts.

The Bearss maps show the location of "B, Sumter" on the morning of

September 17 as being between the Hagerstown pike and Smoketown
Road. Also shown is a bty. (which appears on one map as "E, Sumter"
and on another as "A, Sumter") near R. E. Lee's headquarters at the Reel
house. The locations of Cutts's Bty. "D" and Lloyd's Bty. are not shown
on the Bearss maps. It is possible that neither of these batts. was engaged
in the battle (see Manarin 1988, 1:437). It is frustrating that Cutts in his
article (Cutts 1882, 10:430–31) never actually states what his bn. *did* at
Sharpsburg, a failure that leaves unresolved D. H. Hill's statement that
his div. was supported by "near sixty" pieces from Cutts's Bn. Carman
(Studies Antietam, box 3) notes that batts. "A," "B," and "E" were in reserve and not engaged. Alexander (*O.R.*, ser. 27:155) reports that Lloyd
abandoned a 6-lb. SBML and Ross a 12-lb. SBML howitzer during the
retreat from Boonsboro.

Carman states that the bn. consisted of 4 6-gun batts., plus Lloyd's
North Carolina Bty., temporarily attached. The 5 batts. had 30 guns
altogether, but only 18 were engaged on the seventeenth. According to
Carman (Carman MS, 23:35), Lane's Bty. was engaged on the evening of
the sixteenth but not on the seventeenth, and Lloyd's Bty. was not engaged at all.

The 3 batts. in action on the seventeenth had 9 off., 310 EM=319
aggregate, according to Carman (ibid., p. 25). He notes (ibid., 24:12) that
Cutts's Bn. "suffered severely," losing 2 KIA, 32 WIA=34. The break-
down by bty. is given below (Pendleton 1862; Alexander 1989; Cutts
1882).

Ross's (A, Sumter Arty. Bn., a.k.a. Sumter Flying Arty.) GA
Bty., Capt. Hugh M. Ross: 3 10-lb. Parrott RML, 1 12-lb. SB
howitzer, 1 12-lb. Napoleon SBML.
BC were 18 WIA.

Patterson's (B, Sumter Arty. Bn.) GA Bty., Capt. George M.
Patterson: 3 12-lb. SB howitzers, 3 6-lb. SBML.
Note that in Pendleton's report this armament is that given for Blackshear's Bty. However, this bty. had been disbanded (Special Orders no.
209, ANV [*O.R.*, ser. 28:652–54]) by the time of Pendleton's report and
the men had been assigned to Ross's, Lane's, and Patterson's cos. (*AOCS*
1889, p. 128). It is believed that, at that time, Blackshear was in tempo-
rary command of Patterson's Bty.
BC were 1 KIA, 5 WIA=6.

Blackshear's (D, Sumter Arty. Bn.) GA Bty., Capt. James Ap Blackshear: 5 U/I.
BC were 1 KIA, 7 WIA=8. (See also S. D. Lee's Bn.)

Lane's (E, Sumter Arty. Bn.) GA Bty., Capt. John Lane: 3 10-lb. naval Parrott RML, 1 12-lb. Whitworth BLR, 2 U/I.
Alexander's entry for Oct. 11 mentions that 2 20-lb. Parrott RML were enroute to Lane's Bty. from Richmond. On Oct. 15 Alexander advises Lane to retain the 3-in. (10-lb.) *naval* Parrotts in his bty. Carman notes that the bty. was present but not engaged on the seventeenth (Carman Papers, 15:5).
BC were 2 WIA.

Lloyd's (G [1st Company], 3rd Arty. Rgt.) NC Bty. (attached to Cutts's Bn. from Ransom's Bde.), Capt. W. P. Lloyd: 2 12-lb. SB howitzers, 1 6-lb. SBML.
Manarin (Manarin 1988, 1:437) noted it as present but not engaged. The bty. was disbanded Oct. 4, 1862 (Special Orders no. 209, ANV [*O.R.,* ser. 28:652–54]).

H. P. Jones's Bn., Maj. Hilary Pollard Jones:
Wise (Wise 1959, p. 298) gives Jones's Bn. as 14 guns. But Jones stated to Carman that his battalion consisted of 4 4-gun batteries, 16 guns aggregate, and 12 off., 290 EM=302 (Carman MS, 23:35). Carman (ibid., 24:12) gives Jones's BC as 2 KIA, 15 WIA=17 TBC, but he had no information for Turner's and Wimbish's batts.

Page's (Morris "Louisa") VA Bty., Capt. Richard Channing Moore Page: 4 12-lb. SB howitzers (Page 1885).
Pendleton gives the bty.'s armament as 2 3-in. Ordnance RML, 1 12-lb. SB howitzer, and 3 6-lb. SBML, but Page states (ibid.) that Fredericksburg was the first battle in which the bty. had 6 guns.
Page's BC were 2 KIA, 7 WIA=9 (Carman MS, 24:12), or 1 KIA, 7 WIA, 1 PW, and 2 MIA (1 KIA?)=11 (Macaluso 1991, p. 12).

Peyton's (Richmond "Orange") VA Bty., Capt. Jefferson Peyton: 1 3-in. Ordnance RML, 1 12-lb. SB howitzer, 3 6-lb. SBML.
Peyton's BC were 8 WIA (Carman MS, 24:12), or just 1 WIA (Macaluso 1991, p. 18; Pendleton 1862).

Wimbish's (Long Island) VA Bty., Capt. Abram Wimbish.

Turner's (Co. D, Wise Legion Arty.) VA Bty., Capt. William H. Turner.
Wimbish's and Turner's batts. together had 5 or 7 guns, depending on whether the bn. had 14 or 16 guns. Both batts. were disbanded Oct. 4, 1862 (Special Orders no. 209, ANV [*O.R.*, ser. 28:652–54]).

Unattached Arty.:

Page's (Yorktown "Magruder") VA Bty., Capt. Thomas Jefferson Page, Jr.: unknown.
The bty. was disbanded Oct. 4, 1862 (Special Orders no. 209, ANV [*O.R.*, ser. 28:652–54]).

Cav. Div., Stuart Horse Arty.:
Maj. John Pelham: The batts. of the Stuart Horse Arty. had been frequently and closely engaged in the fighting preceding Antietam and were much run down by the seventeenth. Only Pelham's Bty. played a significant role in the battle.

Carman notes that of the 3 batts. of the Horse Arty., "but 4 guns of Pelham's Battery were engaged" at Antietam (Carman MS, 23:12). This statement may not be correct (see below).

Pelham's (1st Stuart Horse Arty.) VA Bty., Maj. John Pelham: 2 3-in. Ordnance RML, 1 12-lb. Napoleon SBML, 5 U/I.
That Pelham's Bty. had 8 pieces is established from the Chew Papers, "Organization and Roster of McGregor's Bty." (D. Cardwell to Maj. H. B. McClellan, item 41): "The Stuart Horse Artillery was organized in the fall of 1861, with John Pelham, of Talladigo [*sic*], Alabama as Captain. They had eight (8) guns. On the night after the battle of Sharpsburg, before we crossed the rive[r] it was divided into two (2) four (4) gun batteries, with Will McGregor as Captain of one and James Breathed of the other."

Shreve's MS (Chew Papers, p. 7) states that Pelham's Bty. had 6 guns at its organization and provides identification of 3 of Pelham's 8 pieces. The two rifles were spoils of war taken at Manassas Junction on August 27: "From the captured stores we selected two 3 in. rifle guns, and abandoned the two howitzers. These captured guns did good service in our Battery through the war" (ibid., p. 2).

The Napoleon served through the Chancellorsville campaign, when, according to Shreve (ibid., p. 23) it was "burried." Shreve remarks that it "did splendid work, on many a field; but it was always considered too heavy for our flying batteries, especially as our horses were not always the best."

Shreve also states (ibid., p. 4) that Pelham was engaged on the left on the sixteenth, "late in the evening, and also on the next day."

Hart's (Washington) SC Bty., Capt. James F. Hart: 4 12-lb. Blakely RML (Brooks 1912, p. 251).

The bty. had largely exhausted its ammunition in the cavalry fighting for the Catoctin Mountain pass (Braddock Heights) and at Middletown preceding the Battle of South Mountain. This "prevented a very active participation by the battery in the Battle of Sharpsburg" (ibid.).

Hart told Carman that he was ordered across the Potomac at 10 A.M. and placed his guns in position on the south bank covering Boteler's Ford. He stated, "I was using Blakely guns, and had exhausted the supply of shells for these guns, and having a good supply of canister in reserve, I was placed where (in my opinion at the time) if our lines had been forced back, I could use my short-range ammunition effectively" (Studies Antietam, Hart to Carman, March 24, 1900, box 3).

Chew's (Ashby) VA Bty., Capt. Roger Preston Chew: 2 (possibly 3) 3-in. Ordnance RML, 1 Blakely RML, 1 12-lb. SB howitzer.

The Blakely RML broke a trail at Crampton's Gap. This particular gun "ended its life" at Brandy Station, where it fired 160 rounds (Chew Papers, George M. Neese to R. P. Chew, Dec. 3, 1912, item 24).

Identification of Chew's pieces is (haphazardly) established by Chew's statement that after Brandy Station the bty. "had three, three inch rifles . . . and one twelve pound howitzer. We got the howitzer on the 30th of December 1861, and it was along on the Bath trip" (ibid.).

However, McDonald (McDonald 1907, pp. 30–31) notes that at its organization (Nov. 11, 1861) the bty. had 4 off., 33 EM, and 3 guns: 1 Blakely, 1 howitzer, and 1 6-in. RML. The bty. was associated with Ashby's command, the "Laurel Brigade," and was the first bty. of horse arty. in the Confederate Army.

Chew's Bty. does not appear to have been engaged at Antietam. It was camped near Shepherdstown until about 3 P.M. on the seventeenth. At that time, according to Neese, "our first gun [the Blakely] arrived from the repair shop at Martinsburg ready for service. Soon after the gun arrived the battery started for the front. . . . It was about sunset when we arrived on the battlefield, and the sound of the last shot had died away"

(Studies Antietam, Neese to Carman, March 15, 1900, box 3). The bty.'s approach march had been delayed because the road was thronged with wagons and ambulances.

Totals:
Carman gives the following totals for the Confederate arty. *engaged* at Antietam:

Longstreet's Wing:	105 guns[1]
Jackson's Wing:	75[2]
Reserve Arty.:	35[3]
Stuart:	4[4]
Total:	**219[5]**

    1. "Longstreet had 115 guns on the field, 105 of which were in action." The total number of artymen serving the 105 guns in action was 1,792 (Carman Papers, 23:29).

    2. The total number of artymen serving Jackson's 75 engaged guns was 1,216 (ibid., p. 34).

    3. The guns of the Reserve Arty. were served by 621 artymen (ibid., pp. 25, 35).

    4. Carman considered that only Pelham's Bty. was engaged but had no data on Pelham's strength. The bty. probably had about 200 men.

    5. The Confederates had "about 4,500 cavalry, including the horse artillery," and 3,629 artymen, with 219 guns (ibid., 14:50). Carman's estimate for the cav. is too high by about 300.

Army of Northern Virginia Artillery
Not at Antietam

Jackson's Div.:

Rice's (8th Star) VA Bty., Capt. William H. Rice: 1 10-lb. Parrott RML, 1 3-in. Ordnance RML, 1 12-lb. Napoleon SBML.
Moore (Moore 1989, p. 71) states, "Being posted at one of the fords in the vicinity of Williamsport and Shepherdstown, the New Market men missed the Battle of Sharpsburg." Rice's Bty. had 107 men on Aug. 31, 1862, and 103 men at the end of Sept. (ibid.). On Sept. 26, 1862, the battery was merged with Wooding's under Special Orders no. 201, ANV (*O.R.*, ser. 28:629; ser. 27:964, Shumaker's rpt.).

Poague's Bty. (1 section), Sgt. Moore: 1 6-lb. SBML.
At Martinsburg.

R. H. Anderson's Div.:

Anderson's (Richmond "Thomas") VA Bty., Capt. Edwin J.
Anderson: unknown.
Assigned to Wilcox's Bde. Aug. 18, 1862 (Owen 1885, p. 100). At
Leesburg; 27 men with the Louisiana Arty. Bn. during the campaign
(Wise 1959, p. 336). Disbanded Oct. 4, 1862 (Special Orders no. 209,
ANV [*O.R.*, ser. 28:652–54]).

D. R. Jones's Div.:

Stribling's (Fauquier) VA Bty., Capt. Robert Mackey
Stribling: 3 12-lb. SB howitzers.
The bty.'s armament is given by Andrus (Andrus 1990, p. 68). At
Leesburg. Alexander (Alexander, Journal, p. 156) notes that the 2 24-lb.
SB howitzers listed with Stribling in Pendleton's tabulation were pieces
captured at Harpers Ferry. They were issued to the bty. on Nov. 4. In
addition, the bty. received 4 new 12-lb. Napoleon SB howitzers from
stores captured at Harpers Ferry (Andrus 1990, p. 73; Pendleton 1862).

Rogers's (Loudoun) VA Bty., Capt. Arthur Lee Rogers: 2 10-
lb. Parrott RML.
At Leesburg. Assigned to Kemper's Bde. Aug. 18, 1862 (Owen 1885,
p. 100). Disbanded Oct. 4, 1862 (Special Orders no. 209, ANV [*O.R.*, ser.
28:652–54; Andrus 1990, pp. 51–58]).

Leake's (Turner) VA Bty., Capt. Walter D. Leake (resigned,
effective Sept. 12): unknown.
At Leesburg. Five men attached to the Louisiana Arty. Bn. during the
campaign (Wise 1959, p. 336). The bty. was assigned to Drayton's Bde.
on Aug. 18, 1862 (Owen 1885, p. 100); it was disbanded Oct. 4, 1862
(Special Orders no. 209, ANV [*O.R.*, ser. 28:652–54]).

Ewell's Div.:

Brown's (4th "Chesapeake") MD Bty., Capt. William Brown:
2 10-lb. Parrott RML, 1 3-in. Ordnance RML.
At Harpers Ferry.

Carrington's (Charlottesville) VA Bty., Capt. J. McD.
Carrington: 2 3-in. Ordnance RML, 2 12-lb. SB howitzers, 2
6-lb. SBML.
At Gordonsville. (RG 109, Co. MR, Sept. 3–Nov. 1, 1862, microcopy 861,
roll 64; Pendleton 1862; Studies Antietam, box 3).

Dement's (1st) MD Bty., Capt. William Dement: 4 12-lb.
Napoleon SBML.
At Harpers Ferry? (Pendleton 1862).

Latimer's (Courtney) VA Bty. (minus 1 section), Capt. Joseph
White Latimer: 2 12-lb. Napoleon SBML.
At Harpers Ferry; Co. MR, Sept.–Oct., 1862, notes that the bty. was
engaged at Harpers Ferry but makes no reference to Antietam (Pendleton
1862).

A. P. Hill's Div.:

Davidson's (Richmond "Letcher") VA Bty., Capt. Greenlee
Davidson: 1 3-in. Ordnance RML, 2 12-lb. Napoleon SBML, 1
6-lb. SBML.
At Harpers Ferry (Pendleton 1862).

Fleet's (Middlesex) VA Bty., Capt. William C. Fleet:
unknown.
At Leesburg; 46 men attached to Woolfolk's, Ancell's, and Marmaduke
Johnson's batts. during the campaign (Wise 1959, p. 336). Disbanded
October 4, 1862 (Special Orders no. 209, ANV [*O.R.,* ser. 28:652–54]).

Latham's (Branch) NC Bty., Capt. A. C. Latham: 2 12-lb.
Napoleon SBML, 2 6-lb. SBML.
At Leesburg (Pendleton 1862).

D. H. Hill's Div.:

Nelson's (Hanover) VA Bty., Capt. George Washington
Nelson: 5 U/I.
At Leesburg. "All our best horses were taken from us and given to the
batteries which were going over into Maryland." This state of affairs
was due to the "laziness and incompetency of our company officers"
(Runge 1961). Disbanded October 4, 1862 (Special Orders no. 209, ANV
[*O.R.,* ser. 28:652–54]).

Reserve Arty. ANV:
(Minus S. D. Lee's, Cutts's, and Jones's bns). Guarding the Potomac
River fords near Williamsport and Shepherdstown (Pendleton 1862;
O.R., ser. 27:837–38, Barnwell's rpt.).

Brown's Reserve Bn., Col. John Thompson Brown: on the Virginia side of the Potomac, guarding the fords near Williamsport (Carman MS, 11:59; Pendleton 1862).

Dance's (Powhatan) VA Bty., Capt. Willis Jefferson Dance: 1 3-in. Ordnance RML, 1 6-lb. SBML.

Watson's (2nd Richmond Howitzers) VA Bty., Capt. David Watson: 2 10-lb. Parrott RML, 1 12-lb. SB howitzer, 1 Hotchkiss RML.
Crutchfield states that the bty. was sent on the seventeenth to Sharpsburg but arrived late and was not engaged. Stuart's rpt. relates that Watson's Bty. and a section of Hupp's Salem Arty. participated in the action at Williamsport on Sept. 19.

Smith's (3rd Richmond Howitzers) VA Bty., Capt. Benjamin H. Smith, Jr.: 2 10-lb. Parrott RML, 2 12-lb. SB howitzers.

Hupp's (Salem) VA Bty., Capt. Abraham Hupp: 2 12-lb. SB howitzers, 2 6-lb. SBML.

Coke's (Williamsburg) VA Bty., Capt. John A. Coke: unknown.
Coke stated that he was ordered across the Potomac to the battlefield on the night of Sept. 17–18, 1862 (Studies Antietam, Coke to Carman, Oct. 6, 1899, box 3).
  Disbanded Oct. 4, 1862 (Special Orders no. 209, ANV [*O.R.*, ser. 28:652–54]).

Nelson's Reserve Bn., Maj. William Nelson: On the Virginia side of the Potomac River, guarding the ford one mile below Shepherdstown. BC in the action at Shepherdstown (Sept. 19) were 3 KIA, 4 WIA=7 (Maurin: 1 KIA, 2 WIA; Huckstep: 1 KIA; M. Johnson: 1 WIA; unidentified batts.: 1 KIA, 1 WIA [*O.R.*, ser. 27:838; Carman MS, 11:59; Pendleton 1862]).

Kirkpatrick's (Amherst) VA Bty., Capt. Thomas Jellis Kirkpatrick: 2 6-lb. SBML, 2 12-lb. SB howitzers.

Huckstep's (1st Fluvanna) VA Bty., Capt. Charles T. Huckstep: 4 6-lb. SBML.
BC in the action at Shepherdstown (Sept. 19) was 1 KIA (*O.R.*, ser. 27:838).

Johnson's (Richmond) VA Bty., Capt. Marmaduke Johnson:
2 6-lb. SBML, 2 12-lb. SB howitzers.
BC in the action at Shepherdstown (Sept. 19) was 1 WIA (ibid.).

Milledge's (Regular) GA Bty., Capt. John Milledge: 3 3-in.
Ordnance RML, 1 Hotchkiss RML, 1 12-lb. SB howitzer.
The Hotchkiss RML listed in Pendleton's rpt. is probably the fourth 3-in.
RML mentioned in Barnwell's rpt.

Pegram's (Richmond "Purcell") (detachment) VA Bty., Capt.
John G. Barnwell: 1 Whitworth BLR.
This was an ad hoc unit formed from personnel of the bty. left at Harpers
Ferry and armed with a gun brought up from Winchester by Barnwell, a
member of Pendleton's staff (*O.R.*, ser. 27:838, Barnwell's rpt.).

Ancell's (2nd Fluvanna) VA Bty., Capt. John J. Ancell: 2
6-lb. SBML.
On the Virginia side of the Potomac River, guarding the ford 4 miles
above Shepardstown. In the arty. reorganization of Oct., 1862 (Special
Orders no. 209, ANV [*O.R.*, ser. 28:652–54]), Ancell's bty. was merged
with Huckstep's. Pendleton's rpt. gives the combined bty. 6 6-lb. SBML.
Subtracting the 4 6-lb. SBML given for Huckstep in Barnwell's rpt.
leaves 2 for Ancell.

Confederate Ordnance Losses
in the Maryland Campaign

At Crampton's Gap:

Carlton's Bty.: 1 12-lb. SB howitzer (broken axle, abandoned
and captured by the skirmishers of the Vermont Bde.).

Chew's Bty.: 1 12-lb. Blakely RML (broken trail, drawn off).

Retreat From Boonsboro:

Ross's Bty.: 1 12-lb. SB howitzer (broken axle, abandoned).

Lloyd's Bty.: 1 6-lb. SBML (broken axle, abandoned).

Sharpsburg:

Read's Bty.: 1 3-in. Ordnance RML (broken axle, recovered); 1 6-lb. SBML (disabled, recovered).

Moorman's Bty.: 1 10-lb. Parrott RML (broken axle, recovered).

Garden's Bty.: 2 U/I (1 carriage destroyed, 1 damaged, both recovered).

Woolfolk's Bty.: 1 12-lb. SB howitzer; 1 6-lb. SBML (abandoned). These guns were captured by the 28th PA of Tyndale's Bde. (XII Corps) in the plowed field between Mumma's house and the East Woods. The capture of the 12-lb. SB howitzer was credited to Knap's bty. A postbattle note of Brig. Gen. Alpheus S. Williams (comdr., XII Corps) to Col. Henry J. Hunt remarks, "The iron twelve pounder howitzer & caisson Richmond manufacture are now in possession of Capt. Knapp's Penna. Battery it was found on the field [sic]" (Hunt Papers, container 7).

Brockenbrough's Bty: 1 12-lb. Blakely RML (broken trail, recovered); 1 10-lb. Parrott RML (disabled, recovered).

Poague's Bty.: 1 10-lb. Parrott RML; 1 12-lb. Napoleon SBML (disabled, both recovered).

Cutshaw's Bty.: 1 3-in. Ordnance RML (disabled, recovered).

Bondurant's Bty.: 1 U/I (dismounted, recovered).

Shepherdstown:

Maurin's Bty.: 1 10-lb. Parrott RML (abandoned; the capture was credited to Hazard's Bty. D, 5th U.S., which had lost the piece at First Bull Run [Hunt Papers, container 7]).

Milledge's Bty.: 1 12-lb. SB howitzer (abandoned; the gun had originally belonged to the Virginia Military Institute Cadet Bty.).

M. Johnson's Bty.: 1 12-lb. SB howitzer (abandoned).

Huckstep's Bty.: 1 6-lb. SBML (abandoned).

Total lost: 9.
Total damaged/disabled: 12 (all recovered).

Federal Artillery Captured

Harpers Ferry (*O.R.*, 51:548):

6 24-lb. SB howitzers (2 to Stribling, Nov. 4).
4 20-lb. Parrott RML (2 to Poague, Oct. 26; 2 to Rhett?).
6 12-lb. SBML.
6 6-lb. SBML.
2 12-lb. Napoleon SBML.
10 3-in. Ordnance RML.
6 3-in. James RML.
2 10-in. Dahlgren SBML (spiked).
1 50-lb. Parrott RML (spiked).
2 12-lb. Napoleon SBML (spiked).
2 12-lb. SBML (spiked).

Sharpsburg (*O.R.*, ser. 27:963):
1 10-lb. Parrott RML (from Knap's Bty.; capture was credited to D'Aquin's Bty.).

6

Union After-Action Reports

Except as noted (Graham's rpt), none of the following AARs was included in the *Official Records*. They were found among the Hunt Papers at the Library of Congress.

Rpt. of Capt. William M. Graham, Bty. K,
1st US Arty., of the Battle of Antietam

[Ed. note: An AAR of Graham is printed in *OR*, 27:343–344. It is dated 4 Oct 1862 and is addressed to Col. Fred. T. Locke, Army Adjutant General, HQs V Corps. Its wording is slightly different from that given below, and it does not include Graham's list of material losses. However, it does include a paragraph detailing minor activities of the battery on the 18th and 19th, not given in the AAR below.]

Camp near Sharpsburgh, Md.
September 27th, 1862

Sir: I have the honor to submit the following report of the participation of Light Battery K, 1st Artillery, under my command in the action of the 17th at the Antietam.

I was ordered by General Fitz John Porter to report to General Richardson commanding Division in Major General Sumner's Corps about noon. I immediately proceeded to General Richardson's centre and was informed by that officer that his Division was heavily pressed by a large force of Infantry and one Battery and by his direction came into position on the ploughed ground occupied by Genl. Meagher's Brigade in the morning. Here I engaged one of the enemy's brass batteries at seven hundred yards, silenced and drove him away in about ten minutes. At this time two heavy columns of the enemy's Infantry moved upon the Battery, getting within a few hundred yards of my guns, before being discovered by approaching through a heavy cornfield. A very heavy fire of Spherical Case & Shell was opened upon these troops immediately, which in a short time drove them from the field with great slaughter to the woods in their rear. A very sharp fire of Shot, Sph^l. Case & Shell was now opened upon my Battery by two of the Enemy's batteries of rifled guns, one of which enfiladed me. I returned this fire as rapidly as possible, but after firing some twenty minutes, found [that] they were beyond my range, my solid shot falling short several hundred yards, and having called Genl. Richardson's attention to this fact was told by him, that he wished me to save the Battery as much as possible in order that it might advance with his Division at a signal then expected from Major Genl. Sumner. While communicating this to me, Genl. Richardson was mortally wounded by a ball of a Sph[l]. Case from the battery enfilading mine. After this I continued my fire some five minutes, and then retired over the crest of the hill to a point two hundred yards in rear of my first position. I then returned and brought off two of my caissons which were necessarily left at first, the horses being all killed, and having brought all of the wounded off, I re-packed the limbers of the pieces and sent two caissons to the Ammunit[n]. Supply train to be re-filled. My loss in this engagement was:

4 men Killed
5 men Severely wounded
17 Horses killed
6 Horses severely wounded some of which will probably die of the effects of their wounds.

My loss in material was:
192 rounds Ammunition expended
2 Two Trail Handspikes (broken)
5 Five Wheel Traces (do.)
1 one Prolonge
1 one Breech Sight
3 three Whips (driver's)
2 Two Sabres & Belts
4 four Sets Lead Harness (single)
5 five Halters & Straps
5 five Nose Bags
2 two pairs Spurs & Straps

The officers and men behaved without an exception with perfect coolness, and I beg leave to mention particularly Lieuts. Elder, Maynadier & Michalowski, 1st Sergeant Cooney, Serg[ts] Regan & Boyd & Corpl. Walsh. Lieut. Elder served his Section with remarkable effect and was principally instrumental in silencing the Battery first engaged. [H]is conduct under an extraordinary heavy fire was cool and gallant in the extreme. Lieut. Maynadier returned with 1st Serg[t]. Cooney and brought off the two caissons under a heavy Artillery fire. Lieut. Michalowski for a long time served one of his pieces with but one cannoneer, alternating with this man in loading and firing. Some of my fuzes cut for five seconds burst at the muzzle of the guns.

In closing this report I feel called upon to mention the conduct of a citizen (a M^r.) who resides near the battle field. This gentleman drove his carriage to my battery while under a severe Artillery fire and carried off my wounded who were suffering very much for the want of proper surgical attendance and distributed ham & biscuit among the men of the battery. He also returned a second time to the battery. [One] of his horses was wounded while performing this service.

I am, Sir, Very respectfully, Your obedt. Servant,

W. M. Graham,
Captain, 1st Art^y.
Com^dg. Lt. Battery "K"

Col. Henry J. Hunt,
Chief of Artillery

Rpt. of Capt. John C. Tidball, Bty. A, 2nd US Arty., of Operations, Sept. 14–20, 1862

Camp near Shepherdstown, Va.
September 21st, 1862

Sir: On the evening of the 14th inst. I received Orders to report with my battery at daylight the next morning to Brig. Genl. Pleasanton [*sic*] at the village of Boliver [*sic* for Bolivar], Md. near which the battle of South Mountain was fought. Reporting as directed I was at once started with the 9th [*sic* for 8th] Regt. Ills. Cavalry in pursuit of the enemy who were flying in the direction of Boonsboro and Sharpsburg. Taking the turnpike road to the former place I came up with the enemy about a mile beyond it, and a few minutes after our Cavalry had had a severe Skirmish with a greatly superior number of those of the enemy. Bringing several of my pieces into battery a few Shells soon caused the enemy to break from this momentary halt, and after a short pursuit of them our Column turned to the left in order if possible to intercept some who had taken other roads in that direction. A Circuitous march of Several miles brought us upon the turnpike road leading from Boonsboro to Sharpsburg and a few miles from the latter place. Hastening on I soon came up with Richardson's Division which had halted near the bridge over Antietam Creek beyond which and near to the town of Sharpsburg the enemy were posted in great force. In a few minutes they opened a fire of Artillery; upon which I brought my pieces into position, on the crest of a hill to the right of the road, and fired in reply. This drew the fire from four different parts of their line which was all concentrated on my battery, the only one then there. From this time (about 12 m) [12 noon] until dark, at intervals

this firing was kept up; in which practice I always had the last shot.
Early on the morning of the next day I withdrew my guns behind the
crest of the hill and their places were occupied by some of the heavy batteries of the Reserve Artillery. I remained in this position until in the afternoon when I withdrew entirely out of Range.

The next morning—the 17th—the general engagement commenced.
About 10 A.M. I was ordered to cross the turnpike bridge over the Antietam where I took a position on the right of the road. In front the enemy's
Sharpshooters were posted and there being no infantry at hand to drive
them back, I opened fire upon them with Canister, and gradually worked
my guns by hand up a steep ploughed field to the crest of the hill where I
placed them in a commanding position not only for the enemy directly in
front, but for an enfilading fire in front of Sumner's Corps on the right
and that of Burnside on the left of me. The enemy's batteries all the
while were very active, but with some exception his practice was bad.
This exception was upon a section which for a short time I placed in the
road. Taking advantage of every appearance of the enemy I continued firing until about 1 o'clock when my ammunition being well spent, I was
directed by the General to withdraw and replenish; which I accordingly
did and resumed my former position in about two hours. A short time
before sundown I advanced a section to the crest of a hill several hundred
yards further to the front and in front of the infantry of Hancock's brigade. This was a most favorable position for operating on a battery then
in full play upon the center of Sumner's line, and I think that my fire
contributed in no small degree towards the silencing of this battery. Soon
after nightfall I withdrew, by order of the General, from the field, leaving
my position in possession of our infantry.

On the morning of the 19th inst. I was again ordered in pursuit [of
the] enemy who had fled across the Potomac. Arriving near where the
turnpike crosses the river just below Shepherdstown, the head of our column came under fire of the enemy's batteries posted on the opposite of
the river. I moved my battery well forward and in a few minutes brought
my pieces into battery on the left of the road where I had an excellent
fire upon those of the enemy. After a duel of about an hour's duration the
enemy were driven from their Guns, when I withdrew. The next morning
I was again ordered to the front for the purpose of accompanying other
troops in the passage of the river. The force and arrangement for this
purpose being entirely inadequate, those who crossed were soon driven
back and the only part taken by my battery in this unfortunate affair was
to gain a position as quickly as possible on the heights to the left of the
road and from there assist in covering the recrossing of our troops.

Notwithstanding the severe fire to which my battery has upon the oc-
casions mentioned been exposed, it has been exceedingly fortunate in re-
ceiving but little damage. On the 17th I had one private—Hitz killed, and

one severely and two slightly wounded and 10 horses killed. I fired in all about 1200 rounds.

My Officers were Lieutenants Pennington, Dennison, and Clarke, all of whom performed their duties with their usual skill and zeal. My non-commissioned officers and privates likewise performed their duty in the most commendable manner.

[Note: At this point the handwriting changes from that of a copyist to Tidball's own.]

By way of appendix to the above report (which is a copy of the one made to Genl. Pleasonton) I beg leave to add that the use of horse batteries being a new thing in our service, does not appear to be very well comprehended by those [indistinct] whose command they most frequently [indistinct]. The duties assigned to these batteries at the battle of Antietam could have been performed as well by any other batteries, several of which were close by unemployed. This would have left the horse batteries free for rapid movement to any part of that extended field where a concentration of artillery fire was hastily required.

If, when the crisis arrived, and batteries were so much required on the left, the whole twenty-four guns of the horse batteries had been thrown upon that flank a complete, instead of a [indistinct] victory would probably have been the result.

The employment of these batteries alone with cavalry is a dangerous experiment and will most probably lead sooner or later to the loss of guns. Our cavalry is not armed properly for the support of batteries, which without support are by themselves helpless. Cavalry for operating with horse artillery should be armed with muskets or rifles of long range, and should dismount and fight as infantry, their horses being used only for locomotion. As it is and particularly in the instances mentioned in the foregoing report, as soon as the enemy open fire the cavalry finding themselves of no service naturally and very properly retire. This where there is no infantry at hand leave the batteries at the mercy of any enterprising party of the enemy.

Very Respectfully
Your Obt. Svt.
J. C. Tidball
Capt. 2nd Regt.
cmdg. Horse battery A.

1st Lieut. E. R. Warner[1]
Asst. to Chief of Art. A. P.

1. Hunt notes, *OR,* 27:207, that Warner was "the only officer on my staff" (eds.).

Rpt. of Lt. Charles P. Muhlenberg, Bty. A,
5th US Arty., of the Battle of Antietam

Camp near Sharpsburg, Md.
September 21st, 1862

Sir: I have the honor respectfully to make the following report of the part Battery A, 5th Artillery [indistinct] in the engagement of September 17[,] 1862.

[On the] morning of Sept. 17th, '62, by your orders, I put my Battery in position, on the crest of a hill on the east side of the Antietam creek, and some four or five hundred yards from its bank, for the purpose of assisting in covering the crossing of a portion of the troops, composing the left wing of our Army. In obedience to orders received from you, I immediately opened fire upon the woods, to the right and left of the bridge, for the purpose of dislodging the enemy.

After I had kept up a continuous fire some two hours, our Infantry, that up to this time had been stationed in the woods to my right, advanced. When within about fifty yards of the road running along the bank of the stream they were met by a steady fire from the enemy.

I again opened upon the woods, with shell and spherical case, directing my fire entirely upon those points around the bridge, in which I supposed the enemy to be concealed. I had not done so long, before I discovered them leaving the woods, and crossing the fields beyond. The enemy now opened upon me with rifled guns, but at such long range that I deemed it useless to reply. My attention was then called to a column of the enemy's troops, advancing in the direction of the bridge, from a road some distance to my left. They continued to approach, until they were hid from my view [by] a corn field on my left. I threw solid shot into this field [for] the purpose of dislodging them. That I did not succeed the events of the latter portion of the day fully proved. I feared to use any other kind of projectile, as our troops at this time were moving over the bridge.

My firing while at the bridge, with a very few exceptions, was directed entirely at the enemy's troops; the projectiles used were shell, solid shot, and spherical case; the range [indistinct] four and five hundred yards. The shell fired, owing to some defect, I found to be of very little service. In many cases they burst, some at, others not more than fifty yards from, the piece. I experienced no difficulty with my spherical case and expended most of my ammunition, with the exception of canister. I sent my caissons to the rear, to be filled.

About 3 O'clock, P.M., of the same day, I again received orders from you to cross the bridge, with the Battery, and report to Gen[l]. Cox, commanding the 9th Army Corps. He directed me to report for orders, to

Genl. Rodman, in command of the 3r^d Division of his corps. I found him at the front, and was ordered to bring up the Battery, and open fire upon a Brigade of the enemy, that had already outflanked us on the left. When I reached the ground, the enemy had already compelled our forces to fall back, and were within some six hundred yards of the Battery. I came into position, and opened upon him with spherical case and shell. At this time two of our rifled Batteries upon my left, retired from the field. I held my position until I found that I was without a single man to support the Battery, and the enemy within an hundred yards of the guns. I then changed ground to the rear and left. I had no sooner done this than [two] rifled Batteries, one on my left, and the other on my front, opened upon me. The forces of the enemy showing themselves upon my left flank, I directed a section of the Battery against them. Here I again found that the Infantry support, that had been promised me, had not arrived. Feeling, that without support, that the position I held would either result in the capture of the Battery by the forces of the enemy on my left flank, or in its [being?] entirely disabled by the fire of the enemy's guns, I retired from the field. I then, by your orders, again occupied my old position upon the hill commanding the bridge. My officers, 2nd Lt. Geo. W. Crabb and 2nd Lt. Albert [M.?] Murray, did their duty in the best manner, and the conduct of the men could not have been excelled. With this report will be found a statement of casualties to men and horses, and also the amount and kind of ammunition used.

I am Sir,
very respectfully
Your obt. Servant,
Chas. P. Muhlenberg,
1st Lieut. 5 Arty.
cmdg. Battery A.

Lt. Col. Geo. W. Getty,
    Chief of Artillery
        Burnside's Army

Rpt. of Capt. J. R. McMullin, 1st Bty., Ohio Light, of the Battle of Antietam

1st Battery Ohio Artillery
September 19, 1862

Sir: I herewith submit a statement of the action of my Battery in the battle of [the] day before yesterday, 17th inst.

Between 10 and 11 o'clock, I was ordered by Col. Getty, [Chief] of Artillery, to take position near, and about one hundred and fifty yards from, the Bridge on the left of our line of battle, and engaged a force of the enemy, comprising infantry and artillery, posted at a distance of some 1,800 to 2,000 yards, using shell upon them with marked effect. I remained in this position, firing slowly, because of scarcity of ammunition, but as advantageously as possible, until about 3 o'clock, when I removed my pieces from the field, it being impossible to procure ammunition of the calibre of my guns—3^{800} inch.

During the day, Henry Riber, of Co. H, 12th Reg. O. Vols., on detached duty with the Battery, was instantly killed by a 6 pd. round shot passing through the body.

I also had one horse killed, and a gun wheel shattered.

> Very respectfully, etc.
> Your obdt. sev't.
> J. R. McMullin
> Capt. 1st Battery Ohio Artillery

Col. E. P. Scammon
  comd'g Kanawha Division—

Rpt. of Capt. Emory Upton, Chief of Artillery, 1st Div. (Slocum's), VI Corps, of the Battle of Antietam

[Ed. note. Parts of the text of this AAR are missing because of tears or deterioration of the document.]

> Headquarters Artillery Brigade
> Maj. Genl. Slocum's Division, 6th Corps
> Camp near [indistinct], Sep. 26, '62

General: I have the honor to [submit the following] report of the part taken by the [artillery of the] division in the Battle of Antietam.

Arriving near the field [indistinct] we halted until the infantry had formed on the ground previously occupied by Maj. Genls. Meade and Sumner—it was then brought forward to the wood occupied by our troops.

About half past two P.M. I was ordered by Maj. Genl. Slocum to post the batteries and to commence shelling the wood about six hundred yards in our [word missing, may be "front"], which was reported to be filled with the enemy.

Williston's battery (light twelves) was posted nearly within canister range of the wood and on the left of the road intersecting the turnpike at the brick school house [i.e., the Dunkard church]. Wolcott's battery (3-in. Ordnance) was on the right of this road and about 300 yards retired. Porter's battery (light twelves) was placed on Wolcott's right. Williston, as soon as in position, commenced shelling the wood. He was soon replied to by a rebel rifled battery, which was beyond his range. Relieved by Hexamer's battery 10-pdr. Parrotts. [indistinct] fire upon the enemy's battery and by the [indistinct] and accuracy of his fire drove them from the field, in about twenty minutes. Another battery attempted to come into position, but retired under [indistinct] without unlimbering. About 4 P.M. [indistinct] was ordered to Gen. Hancock, I saw nothing more of his [indistinct, possibly "battery during"] the day.

An [indistinct] from the enemy being apprehended, [indistinct] Williston to occupy his former position. He was [indistinct] attacked by a battery near the position of the first. He fired his longest fuzes (5 seconds) but all his shells burst short, and with the greatest elevation his round shot also fell short. I therefore replaced him by Wolcott's battery (rifled), which maintained the contest until dark, when the enemy was silenced or moved on.

About 5.30 P.M. I rode to the left of Col. Irving's [i.e., Irwin's] brigade and there saw a rebel regiment drawn up in line of battle and that could be enfiladed from that position. I ordered forward four of Wolcott's guns; before he could get them into position, the enemy withdrew from his original position and approached to within 700 yards. Wolcott maintained a steady and effective fire upon him until relieved by Williston's light twelves. Williston opened fire with spherical [case] [indistinct] and soon drove the rebels from the field. [Colonel Irwin] in his official report speaks in the highest terms of both [batteries]. He claims that their timely arrival [prevented an?] attack on our lines. After dark all the [batteries were] withdrawn except Capt. Porter's which [remained in position] during the night.

The fire of the artillery [from my own] observation and what I could learn from others was very effective. The commanders of batteries, Captains Hexamer and Wolcott and Lt. Williston, displayed great coolness and judgement in maneuvering their batteries and delivering their fire. They all speak in the highest terms of the conduct of their officers and men.

I would recommend to your notice as being in the regular service 1st Lt. E. Williston, comd'g. Co. D, 2nd Arty., and 2nd Lieuts. H. Borrowe [?] and C. N. Warner. I can bear witness to their coolness and gallantry when exposed to both heavy infantry and artillery fire. Lt. Robert S. Irwin, actg. adjutant, and Sgt. Milbury Green, both of the 1st Mass. Arty., behaved gallantly and were of great service in bearing orders to different parts of the field. For the details of the part taken by each battery, I respectfully refer to the enclosed official reports.

Capt. Porter makes no report, as he was not engaged.

I have the honor,
Respectfully,
Your obt. Svt.

E. Upton
Capt. [indistinct] and Chief of Arty.

Rpt. of Lt. Edward B. Williston, Bty D, 2nd US, of the Battle of Antietam

Battery "D" 2nd U.S. Artillery
Camp in the field near Williamsport, Md.
September 22nd, 1862

Sir: I have the honor to submit the following report of the part taken by this battery in the action near Sharpsburg, Maryland, on the 17th inst.

The battery, which had marched from Crampton['s] Gap in the morning, arrived in the woods and halted at that point where Gen. Newton's Brigade was lying, about 2 o'clock P.M.

In about half an hour the battery was ordered forward by Capt. Upton, Chief of Artillery of the Division, and went into battery to the left of the road and right of the grave-yard.

I opened with spherical case on [and] to the right of the school house [i.e., the Dunkard Church] with good effect.

The enemies [sic] sharpshooters took positions in, and near, the school house and became very annoying, but were forced to seek shelter in the woods, by several well directed round shot which passed entirely through the house.

At this moment, a rebel 20 pnd Parrott battery began to fire upon the battery from a position directly in front, and at an estimated distance of 2000 yards.

They fired shell and shot with remarkable precision, inflicting, however, slight damage upon the battery, owing to the superior position it occupied.

I received an order from Capt. Upton to move out of battery, under cover, which I did, relieved by Hexamer's 1st New Jersey Parrott Battery.

Soon after, meeting Capt. Upton, I requested and obtained his permission to again occupy the position, Capt. Hexamer having been ordered to the left of [the line?].

Having been ordered not to open fire, the battery remained silent, until suddenly, a rifled battery in position near the place where the first one which engaged us was situated commenced to fire solid shot and case, which seemed to be directed against the right half of the battery and the Brigade of Gen. Newton on our left.

The fire was immediately returned by the battery, firing with solid shot at our highest attainable elevation.

I observed that all our shot fell short and being satisfied that ammunition would only be wasted by continuing to fire, I ordered the battery to cease firing and reported the result of my observations to Capt. Upton, who ordered Capt. Wolcott's 1st Maryland 3 in Ordnance Battery to relieve me.

The battery moved to the left and out of artillery fire and remained in a comparatively safe position until ordered by Capt. Upton to take position on a crest of a hill near the brigade of Col. Irving [i.e., Irwin] of the 7th Maine.

Arriving at the place designated, I relieved three guns from Capt. Wolcott['s which were there in battery and coming into action commenced to fire spherical case into an orchard about 700 yards distant and which was reported to be filled with a brigade of rebels which had driven the gallant Maine 7th from the orchards a few minutes previous.

The fire from the battery was very rapid, and the case burst as could most have been desired.

The firing ceased in about half an hour although the battery remained in the same position until 10 o'ck P.M.

I have since learned from officers of our own infantry and from those who visited the orchard afterwards, that the fire from the battery was effective in the extreme, the ground being covered with rebel dead and the trees bearing marks of a very severe fire. I also learned from a rebel officer, whom I saw on the 18 inst. under a flag of truce, that the rebel brigade occupying the orchard at the time the battery commenced firing was very badly cut up and obliged to retire.

During the time we were in our last position the battery was under a severe fire from the enemies sharpshooters which resulted only in wounding one man & horse.

This result I attributed solely to the judgement of Capt. Upton, to whom I consider due the greatest credit for ordering the battery forward to a very advanced position at a critical moment and assigning it a position remarkable alike for its advantages for effecting the desired object and its security from the enemies balls.

I cannot too highly commend the officers. Lieuts. Borrowe and Warner of the battery, and Lt. Fitzhugh 1st New York Vol. Arty. and Lt. Pendleton 1st Va. Vol. Arty. attached, for their gallantry and coolness during the action. The non-commissioned officers and men behaved nobly and offered numerous proofs of bravery under a heavy artillery fire and a most galling fire from the rebel sharpshooters to which they were exposed.

Edward Williston
1st Lieut. 2nd U.S. Arty.
Comdg. Battery "D"

Col. Henry J. Hunt, U.S.A.
   Chief of Artillery —
     Army of the Potomac

Appendix A

Strengths and Casualties of the Artillery Component, Army of the Potomac, Antietam, September 17, 1862

	#FG	BC	Str.
I Corps, 1st Div.			
1, NH Light	(6)	(3)	(121)
D, 1 RI	(6)	(18)	(123)
L, 1 NY	(6)	(5)	(84)
B, 4 U.S.	(6)	(40)	(100)
Total	24	66	428
I Corps, 2nd Div.			
F, 1 PA	(4)	(11)	(76)
C, PA Light	(4)	(13)	(45)
Total	8	24	121
I Corps, 3rd Div.			
A, 1 PA Light	(4)	(4)	(90)
B, 1 PA Light	(4)	(2)	(123)
C, 5 U.S.	(4)	(15)	(114)
Total	12	21	327
II Corps, 1st Div.			
B, 1 NY	(6)	(2)	(123)
A and C, 4 U.S.	(6)	(3)	(123)
Total	12	5	246
II Corps, 2nd Div.			
A, 1 RI	(6)	(19)	(120)
I, 1 U.S.	(6)	(6)	(124)
Total	12	25	244

continued

	#FG	BC	Str.
II Corps, Unatchd.			
G, 1 NY	(6)	(5)	(123)
B, 1 RI	(6)	(0)	(131)
G, 1 RI	(6)	(5)	(123)
Total	18	10	377
V Corps, 1st Div.			
3, MA Light	(6)	(0)	(118)
C, 1 RI	(6)	(0)	(118)
D, 5 U.S.	(6)	(0)	(118)
Total	18	0	354
V Corps, 2nd Div.			
E and G, 1 U.S.	(4)	(0)	(118)
I, 5 U.S.	(4)	(0)	(118)
K, 5 U.S.	(4)	(0)	(118)
Total	12	0	354
Arty. Reserve			
A, 1 NY Light	(4)		
B, 1 NY Light	(4)		
C, 1 NY Light	(4)		
D, 1 NY Light	(6)		
5, NY Light	(4)		
K, 1 U.S.	(6)		
G, 4 U.S.	(6)		
Total	34	2	950
VI Corps, 1st Div.			
A, MD Light	(8)	(14)	(123)
1, MA Light	(6)	(0)	(123)
1, NJ Light	(6)	(0)	(123)
D, 2 U.S.	(6)	(2)	(123)
Total	26	16	492
VI Corps, 2nd Div.			
B, MD Light	(6)	(0)	(123)
1, NY Light	(4)	(0)	(123)
F, 5 U.S.	(4)	(0)	(123)
Total	14	0	369
IX Corps, 1st Div.			
8, MA Light	(6)	(1)	(126)
E, 2 U.S.	(4)	(0)	(93)
Total	10	1	219

	#FG	BC	Str.
IX Corps, 2nd Div.			
D, PA Light	(6)	(3)	(123)
E, 4 U.S.	(4)	(3)	(59)
Total	10	6	182
IX Corps, 3rd Div.			
A, 5 U.S.	(6)	(3)	(102)
9 Co., NY Rgtl.	(5)	(0)	(96)
Total	11	3	198
IX Corps, Kanawha Div.			
1, OH Light	(6)	(1)	(129)
KY Bty.	(6)	(6)	(95)
Total	12	7	224
IX Corps, Unatchd.			
L and M, 3 U.S.	(4)	(0)	(97)
L, 2 NY	(6)	(0)	(98)
Total	10	0	195
XII Corps			
G and S			(1)
4, ME Light	(6)	(0)	(104)
6, ME Light	(4)	(0)	(85)
M, 1 NY	(6)	(6)	(124)
10, NY Light	(6)	(0)	(117)
E, PA Light	(6)	(8)	(101)
F, PA Light	(4)	(3)	(79)
F, 4 U.S.	(6)	(0)	(98)
Total	38	17	709
Horse Arty.			
A, 2 U.S.	(6)	(4)	
B and L, 2 U.S.	(4)	(0)	
M, 2 U.S. (-)	(4)	(5)	
C and G, 3 U.S.	(6)	(0)	
Total	20	9	451
Totals	**301**	**212**	**6,440**

Appendix B

Strengths and Casualties of the Artillery Component, Army of Northern Virginia, Antietam, September 17, 1862

	#FG	BC	Str.
Longstreet's Wing			
McLaws's Div. (Cabell's Bn.)			
Manly	(6)	(4)	
Read	(4)	(14)	(75)
Macon	(6)	(0)	
Carlton	(5)	(9)	(27)
McCarthy	(4)	(2)	(33)
Total[a]	25	29	285
R. H. Anderson's Div.			
(Saunders's Bn.)			
Maurin	(6)	(0)	
Huger	(4)	(3)	
Moorman	(3)	(8)	
Grimes	(3)	(5)	
Chapman[b]	(2)	(0)	
Total	18	16	369
D. R. Jones's Div.			
Brown	4	6	81
Walker's Div.			
French	(6)		
Branch	(6)	(15)	
Total	12	15	230
Hood's Div. (Frobel's Bn.)			
Bachman	(6)	(4)	
Garden	(4)	(12)	
Reilly	(6)	(10)	
Total	16[c]	26	304

continued

	#FG	BC	Str.
Longstreet's Wing (continued)			
Evans's Bde.			
Boyce	6	19	115
Washington Arty.			
Squires	(4)	(13)	
Richardson	(4)	(6)	
Miller	(4)	(14)	
Eshleman	(4)	(0)	
Total	16	33	278
S. D. Lee's Bn.			
Woolfolk	(4)		
Jordan	(4)	(3)	
Elliott	(4)		
Eubank	(4)		
Moody	(4)	(28)	
Parker	(4)	(21)	
Total	24	94	318
Totals: Longstreet's Wing	**121**	**238**	**1,980**

Note: Longstreet could have had 121 guns on the field, but it seems likely that only 19 of Cabell's 25 guns were present, and the personnel strength data given reflect this conclusion. Thus, the total number of guns present with Longstreet's Wing was probably 115. Accepting Carman's data for Cabell only (adjusted for Read), 104 of the guns present with the wing were engaged.

[a] Carman believed that Read had 4 guns engaged, but 1 of the 4 was disabled before the bty. commenced fire.

[b] Neither Carman nor Hanson included Chapman in his accounting.

[c] Carman believed Frobel had 18 guns.

	#FG	BC	Str.
Jackson's Wing			
Ewell's Div. (Courtney's Bn.)			
D'Aquin	(3)	(9)	
Johnson	(3)	(11)	(108)
Garber	(2)	(2)	
Latimer	(2)	(0)	
Total	10	22	223
A. P. Hill's Div. (Walker's Bn.)			
Crenshaw	(4)	(5)	
Braxton	(6)	(0)	
McIntosh	(4)	(3)	
Pegram	(4)	(14)	
Total	18	22	337
Jackson's Div. (Shumaker's Bn.)			
Carpenter	(3)	(5)	
Cutshaw	(4)		
Brockenbrough	(4)	(8)	
Wooding	(2)	(15)	(64)
Raine	(4)	(5)	
Poague	(3)	(6)	
Caskie	(1)		
Total	21	39	310
D. H. Hill's Div. (Pierson's Bn.)			
Hardaway	(3)	(9)	
Bondurant	(4)	(9)	
Jones	(4)	(26)	
Carter	(5)	(6)	
Total	16	50	346
Totals: Jackson's Wing	**65**	**133**	**1,216**

continued

	#FG	BC	Str.
General Reserve Arty.			
Cutts's Bn.			
Ross	(5)	(18)	
Patterson	(6)	(6)	
Blackshear	(5)	(8)	
Lane	(6)	(2)	
Lloyd	(3)	(0)	
Total	25	34	443
H. P. Jones's Bn.			
R. C. M. Page	(4)	(11)	
Peyton	(5)	(8)	
Wimbish and Turner	(7)		
Total	16	19	302
Unatchd.			
T. J. Page (est.)	4		68
Cav. Div. (Stuart Horse Arty.)			
Pelham	(8)		
Hart	(4)		
Chew	(4)		
Total	16		400
Totals	**241**	**424**	**4,409**

Appendix C

Ordnance Holdings of the
Armies, Antietam, September 17, 1862

Federal Army of the Potomac

M-1841 32-lb. howitzer	(6)
20-lb. Parrott	(22)
10-lb. Parrott	(57)
M-1841 12-lb. howitzer	(3)
M-1857 12-lb. gun–howitzer	(117)
3-in. Ordnance RML	(81)
12-lb. Dahlgren boat howitzer	(5)
12-lb. James RML	(10)
Total	**301**

Confederate Army of Northern Virginia

M-1841 24-lb. howitzer	(4)
10-lb. Parrott	(43)
M-1841 12-lb. howitzer	(44)
M-1857 12-lb. gun–howitzer	(14)
12-lb. naval howitzer	(2)
3-in. Ordnance RML	(42)
Whitworth gun	(2)
Blakely gun	(7)
M-1841 6-lb. gun	(41)
Unidentified	(42)
Total	**241**

References

Aldrich, Thomas M. 1904. *The History of Battery A, First Regiment Rhode Island Light Artillery*. Providence: Snow and Farnham.

Alexander, E. P. 1862. Extracts from Journal, October 1–November 15, 1862, *O.R.*, ser. 27:153–56. Cited as Alexander.

———. 1989. *Fighting for the Confederacy*. Chapel Hill: University of North Carolina Press.

Allan, William. 1892. *The Army of Northern Virginia in 1862*. Boston: Houghton Mifflin and Co.

———. 1883. "Confederate Artillery at Second Manassas and Sharpsburg." *SHSP* 11, no. 7 (July, 1883): 289–91.

Ames, Nelson. 1900. *History of Battery G, First Regiment New York Light Artillery*. Marshalltown, Iowa.: Marshall Printing Co.

Andrus, Michael J. 1990. *The Brooke, Fauquier, Loudoun, and Alexandria Artillery*. Lynchburg, Va.: H. E. Howard, Inc.

Antietam Battlefield Board Papers. U.S. National Archives, Washington, D.C.

Bearss, Edwin C. 1962. *Troop Movement Maps, Battlefield of Antietam*. U.S. National Park Service.

Birkhimer, William E. 1884. *Historical Sketch of the Organization, Administration, Materiel, and Tactics of the Artillery, United States Army*. Washington, D.C.: James J. Chapman.

———. 1893. "The Third United States Artillery." *Journal of the Military Service Institution of the United States* 14 (1893): 458–80.

Bohannon, Keith S. 1990. *The Giles, Alleghany, and Jackson Artillery*. Lynchburg, Va.: H. E. Howard, Inc.

———. 1988. *The Staunton Artillery: McClanahan's Battery*. Lynchburg, Va.: H. E. Howard, Inc.

Breck, George. 1944. "George Breck's Civil War Letters from Reynolds' Battery." Edited by Blake McKelvey. *Rochester Historical Society Publications* 22 (1944): 91–149.

Brooks, Ulysses Robert, ed. 1912. "Record of Hart's Battery, from Its Organization to the End of the War"; "Sketch of Bachman's Battery"; "Sketches of Hampton's Cavalry, 1861–2–3." In *Stories of the Confederacy*. Columbia, S.C.: State Co.

Brunson, Joseph M. 1927. *Historical Sketch of the Pee Dee Light Artillery, Army of Northern Virginia*. Winston-Salem, N.C.: Stewart Printing House.

Buell, Augustus. 1890. *"The Cannoneer": Recollections of Service in the Army of the Potomac.* Washington, D.C.: The National Tribune.

Carman, Ezra Ayers. Papers and manuscript, "The Maryland Campaign." Manuscript Division, Library of Congress, Washington, D.C.

————, and E. B. Cope. 1908. *Map[s] of the Battlefield of Antietam.* Rev. ed. Washington, D.C.: Antietam Battlefield Board. 14 maps.

Carmichael, Peter S. 1990. *The Purcell, Crenshaw, and Letcher Artillery.* Lynchburg, Va.: H. E. Howard, Inc.

Chamberlayne, Edwin H., Jr. 1883. *War History and Roll of the Richmond Fayette Artillery, 38th Virginia Battalion Artillery, Confederate States Army, 1861–1865.* Richmond: Everett Waddey.

Chew, Roger Preston. Papers. Jefferson County (Charles Town, W.Va.) Museum. Particularly useful in these documents is George W. Shreve's MS "Reminiscences in [*sic*] the History of the Stuart Horse Artillery."

————. 1911. *Military Operations in Jefferson County, Virginia (and West Va.), 1861–1865.* Charlestown, W. Va.: Farmers Advocate Print.

Clark, Gibson. 1943. "Reminiscences of Civil War Days." *Annals of Wyoming* 15 (1943): 377–86.

Clark, Walter, ed. [1901] 1982. *Histories of the Several Regiments and Battalions from North Carolina in the Great War, 1861–'65, Written by Members of the Respective Commands.* 5 vols. Goldsboro, N.C.: Nash Bros., 1901; reprint, Wendell, N.C.: Avera Press, 1982.

Clark, William (comp.). 1909. *History of Hampton Battery F, Independent Pennsylvania Light Artillery. . . .* Akron: Werner Co.

Coggins, Jack. 1962. *Arms and Equipment of the Civil War.* Garden City, N.Y.: Doubleday & Co., Inc.

Cuffel, Charles A. 1900. *Durell's Battery in the Civil War.* Philadelphia: Craig, Finley & Co.

Cutts, Allan S. 1882. "The Number of Guns in Cutts's Battalion at Sharpsburg." *SHSP* 10 (1882): 429–31.

Daniel, Frederick S. 1891. *Richmond Howitzers in the War: Four Years Campaigning with the Army of Northern Virginia.* Richmond: n.p.

Davis, S. R., comp. *Reports of Military Operations during the Rebellion, 1860–1865.* Vol. 6. Washington, D.C.: Adjutant- General's Printing Office, 1874–80. This publication was a forerunner of *O.R.* Cited as *RMO.*

Dawson, Francis W. 1882. *Reminiscences of Confederate Service, 1861–1865.* Charleston, S.C.: The News & Courier Book Presses.

Dillon, Lester R. 1975. *American Artillery in the Mexican War, 1846–1847.* Austin: Presidial.

Dyer, Alexander B. 1890. "The Fourth Regiment of Artillery." *JMSIUS* 11 (1890): 843–67.

[Fishburne], C[lement] D. "Historical Sketch of the Rockbridge Artillery, C. S. Army." *SHSP* 23 (1895), 98–158.

Fonerden, C. A. 1911. *A Brief History of the Military Career of Carpenter's Battery.* New Market, Va.: Henkel & Co.

Furney, L. A., ed. 1897. *Reminiscences of the War of the Rebellion, 1861–1865, by Bvt.-Maj. Jacob Roemer.* Flushing, N.Y.: Estate of Jacob Roemer.

Graves, Joseph A. 1903. *The History of the Bedford Light Artillery.* Bedford City, Va.: Press of the Bedford Democrat.

Hanson, Joseph Mills. 1940. *A Report on the Employment of the Artillery at the Battle of Antietam, Md.* Petersburg, Va.: National Park Service. Cited as Hanson.

Haskin, William Lawrence. 1879. *The History of the First Regiment of Artillery, from Its Organization in 1821.* Portland, Maine: B. Thurston.

"Historical Sketch of the Rockbridge Artillery." 1895. *SHSP* 23 (1895): 98–158.

Hunt, Henry Jackson. Papers. Manuscript Division, Library of Congress, Washington, D.C. Container 7: Military Papers, 1841–62, Dec. 15.

———. "Mem.[orandum] of Field Batteries, in [*sic*] September 10, 1862."

———. Miscellaneous returns, AARs, and other documents.

———. "My First Efforts to Get Together the Artillery of the Army, after Pope's Campaign."

———. Report, Barry to Hunt, camp near Sharpsburg, Sept. 28, 1862.

Johnson, Robert Underwood, and Clarence Clough Buel. [1887] 1956. *Battles and Leaders of the Civil War.* 4 vols. Reprint, New York: Thomas Yoseloff, Inc.

Krick, Robert K. 1986. *The Fredericksburg Artillery.* Lynchburg, Va.: H. E. Howard.

———. 1991. *Lee's Colonels: A Biographical Register of the Field Officers of the Army of Northern Virginia.* 3rd ed., rev. Dayton, Ohio: Morningside.

———. 1975. *Parker's Virginia Battery, C.S.A.* Berryville, Va.: Virginia Book Co.

Lee, Susan Pendleton. 1893. *Memoirs of William Nelson Pendleton.* Philadelphia: Lippincott.

Longacre, Edward G. 1977. *The Man behind the Guns: A Biography of Gen. Henry Jackson Hunt, Chief of Artillery, Army of the Potomac.* South Brunswick, N.J.: Thomas Yoseloff, Inc.

Macaluso, Gregory J. 1991. *Morris, Orange, and King William Artillery.* Lynchburg, Va.: H. E. Howard, Inc.

McDonald, William Naylor. 1907. *A History of the Laurel Brigade, Originally the Ashby Cavalry of the Army of Northern Virginia and Chew's Battery.* Edited by Bushrod C. Washington. Baltimore: Sun Job Print Office.

Manarin, Louis H. 1988. *North Carolina Troops, 1861–1865: A Roster (Artillery).* Vol. 1. Raleigh, N.C.: State Division of Archives and History (Broadfoot Publishing Co.)

Manucy, Albert. 1949. *Artillery through the Ages.* Washington, D.C.: GPO.

Marvel, William. 1985. *The First New Hampshire Battery, 1861–1865.* South Conway, N.H.: The Lost Cemetery Press.

Monroe, J. Albert. 1886. "Battery D, First Rhode Island Light Artillery at the Battle of Antietam, September 17, 1862." *Personal Narratives of the Battles of the Rebellion,* 3rd ser., no. 16 (1886): 1–45.

134   **References**

Moore, Frank, ed. *The Rebellion Record: A Diary of American Events, with Documents, Narratives, Illustrative Incidents, Poetry, etc.* 11 vols. New York: G. P. Putnam, 1861–63; D. Van Nostrand, 1864–68.

Moore, Robert H. II. 1990. *The Charlottesville, Lee Lynchburg, and Johnson's Bedford Artillery.* Lynchburg, Va.: H. E. Howard, Inc.

———. 1989. *The Danville, Eighth Star New Market, and Dixie Artillery.* Lynchburg, Va.: H. E. Howard, Inc.

Naisawald, L. Van Loan. 1960. *Grape and Canister: The Story of the Field Artillery of the Army of the Potomac, 1861–1865.* New York: Oxford University Press.

Neese, George Michael. 1911. *Three Years in the Confederate Horse Artillery.* New York: The Neale Pub. Co.

Nevins, Allan, ed. 1962. *A Diary of Battle: The Personal Journals of Colonel Charles S. Wainwright, 1861–1865.* New York: Harcourt, Brace & World.

Owen, William Miller. 1885. *In Camp and Battle with the Washington Artillery of New Orleans: A Narrative of Events during the Late Civil War from Bull Run to Appomattox and Spanish Fort.* Boston: Ticknor.

Page, Richard Channing Moore. 1885. *Sketch of Page's Battery, Or Morris Artillery, 2nd Corps, Army of Northern Virginia.* New York: T. Smeltzer.

Parker, Foxhall Alexander. 1865. *The Naval Howitzer Ashore.* New York: D. Van Nostrand.

Pendleton, William N. 1862. Report of Sept. 26, 1862, and tabular list of batteries ca. Nov. 7, 1862, *O.R.,* ser. 27:836–37. Cited as Pendleton.

Peterson, Harold L. 1969. *Round Shot and Rammers: An Introduction to Muzzle-Loading Land Artillery in the United States.* Harrisburg: Stackpole.

Poague, William Thomas. 1957. *Gunner with Stonewall.* Jackson, Tenn.: McCowat-Mercer Press.

Reichardt, Theodore. 1865. *Diary of Battery A, First Regiment Rhode Island Light Artillery.* Providence: N. Bangs Williams.

"Roster of King William Artillery." 1896. *SHSP* 24 (1896): 156–57.

Runge, William H., ed. 1961. *Four Years in the Confederate Artillery: The Diary of Private Henry Robinson Berkeley.* Virginia Historical Society Documents, vol. 2. Chapel Hill: University of North Carolina Press.

Schilling, Harry E., Jr. 1949. "The Role of U.S. Artillery in Decisive Campaigns of the Civil War, 1861–1865." Master's thesis, University of Maryland.

Sumner, George C. 1897. *Battery D, 1st Rhode Island Light Artillery in the Civil War, 1861–1865.* Providence: Rhode Island Print Co.

Studies Antietam, U.S. National Archives. RG94. Records of the Adjutant General's Office, 1780–1917. 3 boxes. Washington, D.C.

Thompson, John H. "Shaft to Historic Old Portsmouth Artillery." *SHSP* 34 (1906), 144–55.

U.S. National Archives. RG 109. War Department Collection of Confederate Records.

U.S. War Department. *The War of the Rebellion: A Compilation of the*

Official Records of the Union and Confederate Armies. Vol. 19, parts 1–2, ser. 27–28. *Operations in Northern Virginia, West Virginia, Maryland, and Pennsylvania, Sept. 3–Nov. 14, 1862.* Washington, D.C.: GPO, 1889–90. Cited as *O.R.*

————. *The War of the Rebellion: A Compilation of the Official Records of the Union and Confederate Armies.* Vol. 51, part 1, ser. 107 (supplement). *Reports, Union Correspondence, etc.—Jan. 1, 1861–June 30, 1865.* Washington, D.C.: GPO, 1897. Cited as *O.R.*

U.S. War Department. Rebel Archives Division. *Artillery Organizations of the Confederate States, 1861–1865.* Washington, D.C.: GPO, 1889. Cited as *AOCS.*

Virginia Artillery. Richmond Howitzers. *Contributions to a History of the Richmond Howitzer Battalion.* Richmond, Va.: C. McCarthy & Co., 1883–86.

Wise, Jennings Cropper. *The Long Arm of Lee: The History of the Artillery of the Army of Northern Virginia.* Lynchburg, Va.: J. P. Bell and Co., 1915; reprint, 2 vols. in 1, New York: Oxford University Press, 1959.

Young, Charles P., and Thomas Ellett. 1903. "History of the Crenshaw Battery." *SHSP* (1903): 275–96.

Index

Note: Ranks/grades given are those held at the time of the Battle of Antietam.

137